INDIAN cooking

SAVITRI CHOWDHARY

Foreword by **Jennifer Paterson**

ANDRE DEUTSCH

First published in Great Britain in 1954 by André Deutsch Ltd

This edition first published in 1999 by André Deutsch Ltd
76 Dean Street
London W1V 5HA

www.vci.co.uk

André Deutsch is a VCI plc company

Printed and bound in Great Britain by St Edmundsbury Press, Suffolk

A catalogue record for this book is available from the British Library

ISBN 0 233 99630 3

Design by Kee Scott Associates
Photographs courtesy of The Indian Tourist board, Global Scenes Photographic Library
and Capital Pictures

Contents

INDIAN cooking

Foreword

Millions of people in Britain eat Indian food whether in restaurants, as take-aways, or from supermarkets, packaged up and ready cooked. It seems as if we eat it at a rate of knots, every minute of the day. I think this is because many people like a sameness in their food – lots of people cover anything in front of them with either brown sauce or tomato ketchup – and there is a great deal of sameness in mass produced Indian curries. The same spices are used time and time again. But if you have eaten with Indian friends you will realize that there is nothing samey about Indian food at all.

If you are interested in real Indian food, this nice little edition will put you on the right path. Savitri Chowdhary starts with the methods of serving. There is lots of detail on preparing the basic ingredients such as butter-fat, milk curd or dahi panir (soft milk cheese) and Chowdhary also names the various spices required, all of which can be found in the many Indian stores we now have. Apparently, Indians often start with a sweetish first course, so these are given in the first chapters and are not to be confused with the very sweet sweetmeats which come at the end. Most of the sweetmeats are fried first and then boiled in syrup. There are also tea-time savouries which are much more to my taste.

All the rice dishes, which I love, are carefully described. I often think the Indian rice is the best in the world especially the habit of serving it with crisp brown onion rings and hard boiled eggs on top. It is rather like the English version of Kedgeree, very different from the real 'Khicharhi' which is made with lentils or red beans. There is a good chapter on all the different breads to accompany various dishes, poppadoms, chapatis, unleavened and leavened bread and puffed and fried bread – endless variations.

Ways to prepare hot or cold meat and poultry curries abound together with all the vegetable ones as well. I think the Indians probably produced the best vegetarian diet in the world. Different dishes are subtly spiced and as Savitri Chowdhary points out there is a wide choice of how hot the curries can be. Many are not fiery and if you do your own cooking, you can of course season to your own taste.

Use this book, make you own Indian food and taste the difference.

Jennifer Paterson

*INDIAN*cooking

Introduction to 1999 Edition

My mother, Savitri Devi Chowdhary was born in Multan, now in Pakistan. She had four sisters and a brother and learnt to cook at an early age. She was particularly devoted to her father who was a schoolteacher and she followed him into the profession, before marrying my father and moving to live with his family in Muradpur, a village in Punjab. Soon after their marriage my father came to England. He decided to stay, taking up a post as a general practitioner in the small town of Laindon in Essex. After a four-year separation, my mother joined him in 1932.

Whilst she struggled at times to grasp her totally new way of life as doctor's wife in a small English town, her determination to adapt and prove her worth shone through. Part of this adaptation was to give up being a strict vegetarian and to start eating fish, eggs and meat. She also had her waist length hair bobbed and started to wear western clothes, saving her silk saris for evenings out. She soon became adept at providing my father with an English meal during the day, but made sure that she cooked curry for the evening meal. I recall how these meals would provide the high point of my father's day after a hard time tending to the sick in the surgery. He enjoyed spicy food and as children my brother and I would watch the perspiration appear on his forehead and trickle down his face as he ate with relish, frequently augmenting his main meal with home made hot pickle and raw chillies.

As children my mother made mild curries for us. Even our dog enjoyed left-over curry and was particularly fond of chapatis! Whenever I was feeling below-par, I would ask my mother to cook something tasty. I just adored pakorhas – they gave warm, savoury comfort and had a magical effect. They would raise the spirits of the most woe-begon child. If you had a sweet tooth, then Carrot Halva would have a similarly satisfying result.

My parents became enormously popular in the small town of Laindon and were renown in the local community for contributing so much time and energy in their respective roles. Nothing was too much trouble for my mother – walking along High Road, Laindon to shop took some time if you were with her as she stopped to talk to so many people!

In the 1930s in London, my mother was lured into the campaign for Indian Independence, working with Krishna Menon, a one time St Pancreas Borough Councillor, co-founder of Penguin Books and the instigator of the India League. She attended meetings and was sometimes asked to speak in public, an experience that stood her in good stead in later years when she lectured to organizations on Indian festivals and culture. Her talks included demonstrations on how to put on a sari and invariably concluded with the provision of Indian food.

But it was when mount Everest was being scaled for the first time in the early 1950s, that she first wrote down a recipe. A letter in *The Times* drew her attention to the fact that Raymond Lambert, a mountaineer with Sherpa Tensing, who reached the then highest point of the mountain, always ate a large bowl of semolina pudding whilst on expeditions and considered that because of this, nothing ever went wrong. This prompted my mother, who had by now qualified as a journalist, to respond pointing out that Indian people also enjoyed semolina preparations, in particular Halva. She gave the outline for the recipe. Her letter went on to say, 'This dish is one of the oldest and most popular sweet dishes of India. The elderly ladies firmly believe that this is the best food for giving strength and energy. It is also the favourite sweet dish of the Punjabi Sikhs, who are universally known for their fighting ability, strength and tenacity.' In response my mother received letters from all over the world asking for the full recipe for Halva,

Introduction to this edition

as well as expressing interest in other Indian dishes. This promoted her to set about writing *Indian Cooking*. Research for the book included visits to India to refresh her existing knowledge as well as to discover new dishes. Although the recipes in *Indian Cooking* favour the cooking used in Punjab, they are essentially classic in their method and the ingredients are readily available. The recipes are easy to follow and cater for those who have never cooked Indian food as well as for those of us who are experienced in cooking curries but need guidance on more specialist items such as pickles, chutneys, sweetmeats and savouries.

Although there is now an abundance of Indian restaurants, it is in the home that you find the real flavours of traditional Indian food. I remember being invited to lunch in Kent by acquaintances who had prepared a chicken curry. I remarked how delicious it tasted and how it so reminded me of my mother's chicken curry. I half expected her to appear from the kitchen. The hosts produced a cookery book which they said was full of wonderful things and never failed them. Of course, it turned out to be *Indian Cooking*. I still find it astonishing that, although my mother rarely used written recipes herself, she was able to make it possible for others to reproduce, so perfectly, the tastes of authentic Indian home cooking, so different from what we are used to in restaurant food. Sadly my mother died in 1996. She would of course have been delighted to know of the renewed interest in her book and that her recipes will continue to contribute to the richness of the different cuisines that we now enjoy.

Despite my mother's many other activities she never lost the traditional Indian value that sees food preparation as an expression of love and nurturing of the family. In enjoying the delicious recipes, one not only continues to be nourished by her, but one is also enriched by an essential quality that was an integral part of her.

Shakun Banfield, November 1998

Introduction

An acquaintance of mine once said to me, 'It's no use making curry for my husband, he doesn't like anything hot.' I think many people believe that Indian food is always 'hot'. This is not true. My father, who loved well cooked dishes, never liked chilli powder or ground peppercorn mixed in with his food. It is as well to remember that if you only use turmeric, salt, and a little garam-masala (mixed spices), leaving out the black peppercorns, you can make delicious curries which even small children will enjoy.

Some people hesitate to try Indian cooking because they are not sure whether they can obtain the necessary ingredients. Today, there are Indian grocery stores in most towns which can supply the majority of the ingredients. In addition to this, they are readily available in the larger supermarkets and can also be supplied by mail order. However, I have given substitutes for some things in the course of this book, so that your Indian cooking can still be delicious, even with ingredients obtained entirely from local stores.

There is no need to add curry powder to the recipes. You can also leave out the onions and garlic if you prefer. There are plenty of people in India who do not take onions and garlic.

As a rule, the Indian cook is exceptionally good at guessing the amounts of various ingredients: he/she uses weights and measures only when an extra large quantity of food has to be prepared. I must point out that it is not easy to give accurate measurements for the water used in some of the recipes. Therefore it is advisable to take particular note of the terms 'thick' and 'thin' for batter and syrup; and 'stiff' and 'loose' for pastry and dough. This is even more necessary when halving or doubling the quantity of the recipe. There are no hard and fast rules as to how much flavouring or butter-fat to be used in the different dishes, so a little variation in the measures I have given in this book will not spoil the food in any way.

Most cooking utensils in India are made of tin-plated brass, iron or steel. It is, however, quite possible to cook Indian food in heavy enamel or aluminium saucepans.

Deep, heavy frying pans may be used for cooking dry vegetables, for frying, and for condensing milk.

Indian food, including bread, is usually served hot, although milk curd and its preparations are, of course, served cold. The modern way of serving food is to start with one dish of curry (preferably juicy) with the rice pulao. Then follow the other vegetable and meat dishes, which are eaten with any of the varieties of bread, such as chapatis, puris or parathas. Next comes the sweet, and lastly a bowl of fresh fruit.

INDIAN cooking

The traditional way of serving the food is to have a brass or nickel-plated 'thali' (a medium-sized round tray) for each person. On it are arranged two or more shiny bowls filled with various foods. Chapatis or other kinds of Indian bread are usually placed in the centre of the thalis. Although most people in the larger towns and cities use knives, forks and spoons, a great number of Indian people still eat with their hands. They sip the juicy food from the shiny bowls, and ingeniously manipulate the rest by gathering it up with morsels of bread. The traditional custom, especially in the Punjab, was to start the meal with a sweet dish and this is why I have given the recipes for sweet dishes at the beginning of the book.

Although basically the same, Indian cooking does vary a little from province to province, and as I belong to the Punjab my recipes will naturally favour the cooking methods used there.

The subject of Indian cooking is as vast as the country itself, and in making this attempt I am conscious that I have merely skimmed lightly over the surface. Nevertheless, I hope that this little book will be of some help and guidance to everyone who is interested in Indian cooking.

In conclusion, I must acknowledge that much of the credit for this venture of mine goes to my husband, Dr D.S. Chowdhary, who is a connoisseur of Indian cooking.

My sincere thanks are due to my home-help, Miss Florence Rogers, for her cheerful acceptance of the extra work preparing this book has entailed; and to our friend, Mr H.R.Clapp, for his invaluable help in the arranging and preliminary typing.

An attempt has been made to Standardize certain spellings using R.S.McGregor's *Oxford Hindi-English Dictionary* and the *Panjabi Dictionary* of Bhai Maya Singh. Many traditional spellings like *laddoo* and *pulao* have however been retained. I am grateful to Narindar Saroop CBE, for guidance on certain points.

Savitri Chowdhary

Basic Ingredients

Butter-fat

Butter-fat, or ghee as it is called in India, is made in the following way. Place some butter in a saucepan, and simmer for 1–1½ hours. Remove from the heat and strain through a fine cloth. The ghee thus formed may be stored in glass or earthenware jars and will keep for a long time, with a tendency to crystallize as it is kept. Margarine can also be clarified by the same method and kept in the same way.

In my Indian cooking, I use either or a mixture of both, and have found that one heaped tablespoon of butter-fat, when set, equals 3½ tablespoons (or 1½oz) of liquid butter-fat.

For frying purposes, clarified margarine, cooking fat, dripping, or any edible oil may be used.

Milk-curd or Dahi

The best way to make dahi is to mix a tablespoon of yogurt with 600ml (1 pint) of boiled lukewarm full-fat milk and keep this mixture in a warm place for 12–18 hours. When this mixture is set like a jelly, the curd is ready.

Dahi can also be made by putting 1–2 tablespoons of lemon juice in 600ml (1 pint) of boiled lukewarm milk, and letting it set in the usual way. This method, however, does not bring quite satisfactory results at the first setting, because the curd will be rather thin. But, by using 1–2 tablespoons of this thin mixture again in 600ml (1 pint) or warm milk and letting it set as before, the dahi is greatly improved; and when the process is repeated the next time it should have the right consistency.

In very cold weather, the milk for making dahi should be warmer (not really hot), and the quantity of the curd which you are mixing in should be slightly increased and at the temperature of blood-heat. Some people wrap a piece of blanket round the pot or the jug to give extra warmth. After the dahi is set, it should always be kept in a cool place. In India we make dahi in earthenware pots, but I have found that it retains its flavour fairly well even in china jugs. When using dahi, care should be taken to save a little for making the next lot.

Dahi can be served as it is, while some people prefer it with sugar added. It is readily digested, even by those who are allergic to ordinary milk. Some special cold preparations called raitas are made from it. A traditional cool and refreshing drink called lassi can be made by whisking and diluting the

3

INDIAN cooking

curd and adding a little salt or sugar to it, while in summer some ice may be added as well.

Dahi panir (cottage cheese) may be made by placing the curd in a muslin bag and letting it drip overnight. Some people add a little salt to it when it is ready.

Making Butter from Dahi

Dahi is also used for making butter, which is done every day in many Indian households, particularly in the villages. Very early in the morning one hears the sweet, music-like sound of the curd being churned, which is an exercise in itself. Some women say their long prayers (all from memory) or sing their songs as they churn vigorously. Although it is impossible to obtain the original madhani or mathani (churns) and the earthenware pots that we use for butter-making in India, I have tried (and succeeded) in making butter from dahi made with full-fat milk. Here is a recipe which will make 100g (4oz) of butter. You will need a strong egg-whisk.

Ingredients: 2.3 litres (4 pints) of milk, and 3 tablespoons of dahi.

Method: Boil the milk very gently for 1–2 hours. Remove from the heat and when lukewarm make it into dahi by adding the 3 tablespoons of dahi to it, and keeping in a warm place for 12–18 hours. When ready, transfer into a large strong bowl (not too wide), and in summertime cool the dahi slightly before whisking. This should be done vigorously, as gentle whisking does not give satisfactory results. Keep a jug of water at hand, cold or warm according to the time of year; indeed, in summertime, iced water is preferable. Add some of this water to the dahi from time to time as you churn. At first bubbles will form, then they will gradually change colour and thicken. Whilst the butter is forming, continue to add water, whisking in the middle, keeping the butter to the sides. When it is thick enough to gather, do so with both hands and place it in a bowl of cold water. It will very soon become as thick and solid as ordinary butter. All this should not take more than half an hour. Sometimes a second whisking yields a little more butter but usually it comes all at once.

Butter-milk or whey is the proper Indian lassi, which is commonly used for drinking. It may be used in curries instead of dahi, and is very good in soups.

Panir (Soft Milk Cheese)

There are two methods of making this.

(1) Heat 600ml (1 pint) of milk in a saucepan, and when boiling add to it ½ teacup of curd that has been made a day or two previously. Bring to the boil again, and when solid lumps are formed, strain through a fine cloth. The whey can be used in soups and gravies. Press the bag containing the panir with a heavy weight, so as to squeeze out all the whey.

(2) Bring 600ml (1 pint) of milk to the boil, stirring a little so that all the cream does not come to the top. When the milk rises, add one tablespoon of lemon juice to it; mix well, and as soon as the lumps are formed, strain through a fine cloth and press with a heavy weight, as in the previous method.

Panir is used in making certain sweetmeats, while cubes of panir may be cooked with fresh peas, potatoes or tomatoes.

Khoya (Khoa)

This may be made by boiling milk fairly quickly in a karahi (a shallow iron pot) or in a thick aluminium frying pan for an hour, stirring continuously when it begins to thicken. When cool, the residue is khoya, which becomes like stiff pastry. It is used in many Indian sweetmeats. 600ml (1 pint) of ordinary milk will make just over 50g (2oz) of khoya. Full-fat milk yields a little more khoya than ordinary milk.

Khoya – Made with Full-fat Powdered Milk

I have made khoya by mixing 50g (2oz) of full-fat powdered milk with 1½ tablespoons of hot water, and working this into the same smoothness as ordinary khoya.

Dhania (Corianders)

This herb is very commonly used in Indian cooking, and it can easily be grown elsewhere in kitchen gardens.

Methi (Fenugreek)

This vegetable is also used as a herb in many Indian dishes, especially after it has been dried. It has a delightful fragrance and flavour. Methi, like dhania, can be grown quite successfully.

Parsley, sage, thyme and other herbs may be used if dhania and methi

INDIAN cooking

are not available. The quantity of the herbs used in various dishes should depend on individual taste. If dried herbs are used then the quantity should definitely be much reduced.

Cardamoms

Cardamoms are one of the ingredients of garam-masala, and are used in flavouring and to give sweet fragrance to a great many Indian sweetmeats and curried dishes. They are of two kinds – large dark brown, and small pale green. Either type may be used, though the dark brown variety is mainly used for flavouring sweetmeats. Cardamoms are obtainable from Indian grocery stores and from most supermarkets.

Garam-Masala

The following recipe will make a good jarful of garam-masala.
Ingredients: 50g (2oz) black peppercorns, 50g (2oz) coriander seeds, 40g (1½oz) caraway seeds (preferably black), 15g (½oz) cloves, 20 or more large cardamoms, 15g (½oz) cinnamon.

Method: Sort the peppercorns, coriander seeds, caraway seeds and cloves, and remove the skin from the cardamoms. Mix together, and grind them fairly finely (not powdery) in a coffee grinder (kept separately for grinding spices). Mix in the ground cinnamon, and keep the garam-masala in an airtight jar. Garam-masala is used in most Indian curried dishes, giving extra taste and fragrance to the food. All the ingredients are widely available.

   Ready-to-use garam-masala is sold in Indian grocery stores and some of the larger supermarkets, but the fragrance and taste of home-made masala is well worth the trouble taken.

Besan

This is the name given to flour made from chana dal (a split Bengal pulse). It can be bought from Indian grocery stores, but I have ground yellow split peas and have found that they make an excellent substitute for besan. I have also ground dal urad (a small black bean, split) and red lentils for making mongorhis and papar (poppadoms). The coffee grinder used in making garam-masala will do equally well for this purpose, but should be kept adjusted for finest grinding possible.

Basic Ingredients

Pulses

We use a variety of pulses in India, but the following, which can all be easily obtained from Indian grocery stores and some supermarkets, are those most commonly used in the Punjab.

Whole Urad: A very small black bean, which is used just as it is.
Dal Urad: The whole urad, split. It can be used either with its husk or without it, in which case it is white in colour.
Dal Moong: Very like dal urad, but the husk is green. It, too, may be used with or without its husk, and it cooks quickly. I have found red lentils a good substitute for this.
Kabli Channas: A kind of dried pea, of a pale biscuit colour. There is another kind, dark brown and slightly smaller, which is a good alternative.
Dal Channa: The small brown channas, split. Similar to split peas, which can quite well be substituted for it.

Tamarind (Imli)

Tamarind pulp, or tamarind in syrup, is not suitable for our purpose, but dried tamarind (the proper fruit with fibre and all) can be obtained from the Indian grocery stores and some supermarkets. Sometimes it is slightly gritty, and should be rinsed before using.

Ginger

Fresh ginger, when in season, can be obtained from Indian grocery stores and most supermarkets, and I have found that root ginger, when well soaked beforehand, has almost the same flavour as fresh ginger. Ground ginger is not suitable for Indian preparations.

INDIAN cooking

Sweet Dishes

Semolina Halva

Halva Suji

175g (6oz) sugar
A pinch of saffron
50ml (2fl oz) milk
275ml (10fl oz) water
2½ tablespoons (4oz) set butter-fat

100g (4oz) semolina
2 tablespoons sultanas, well-washed
2 tablespoons almonds, thinly sliced
1½ teaspoons crushed cardamom
*   seeds, or freshly grated nutmeg*

For 4 people

Mix the sugar, saffron, milk and water, and boil for a few minutes; then pour this hot syrup into a jug. Melt the butter-fat in a large saucepan or deep frying pan, mix in the semolina and fry very slowly for about 10 minutes, stirring all the time. When the butter begins to separate from the semolina, and the mixture is a golden colour, it is time to pour in the syrup. Add the sultanas, and boil quickly until all superfluous liquid has dried off, stirring all the time with a large spoon; this should not take more than 10 or 15 minutes. Pour the halva into a shallow heatproof glass or china dish, and decorate it with almonds and cardamom seeds or nutmeg and a pinch of saffron.

Instead of all sugar, I have used 100g (4oz) sugar and 1½ tablespoons golden syrup, and to my mind this improved the flavour.

After it is ready, it can be kept hot in a covered dish in a very low oven for an hour or so. It can be re-heated, which should be done very slowly, so that the halva does not become too stiff.

This halva can be made with wholemeal flour or besan (split pea flour, see page 6) instead of semolina. It is a traditional dish, and a favourite of most Indians. It is considered very nourishing, and goes well with puris – a famous variety of Indian bread. It is usually served hot, although it can be served cold in the summer.

INDIAN cooking

Carrot Halva

Gajar Halva

1.2 litres (2 pints) milk
350g (¾lb) carrots
165g (6½oz) sugar
1 tablespoon golden syrup
1 tablespoon sultanas

2 tablespoons set butter-fat
2 dozen or more almond nuts
1 teaspoon cardamom seeds,
  or grated nutmeg

For 6 people
Boil the milk in a large heavy aluminium sauce-pan. Scrape (not peel), wash and grate the carrots, and put them in with the milk. Cook over medium heat for just over an hour, stirring frequently with a large spoon to prevent sticking; the mixture by then should be fairly thick. Add sugar, syrup, sultanas and the butter-fat; pour the mixture into a deep aluminium frying pan, and keep boiling gently until the mixture begins to solidify, stirring frequently.

When the halva is of a deep orange colour, and has the desired consistency, it should be taken off the heat, spread on a well-buttered heatproof glass or china dish and decorated with the peeled and sliced almonds and the crushed cardamom seeds or nutmeg.

This halva can be served hot or cold, and should keep for three to four days. It is not only delicious, but is considered good nourishing food.

Banana Halva

Kela Halva

1½ tablespoons butter-fat
4 or 5 ripe firm bananas
1¼ teacups water
150g (5oz) sugar
A few drops of vanilla, or other
   flavouring

1 teaspoon crushed cardamom
   seeds or grated nutmeg
2 dozen almonds

For 3 or 4 people
Heat the butter-fat in a heavy aluminium frying pan. After peeling the bananas, cut them into 2.5cm (1in) long pieces, place in the fat and fry over medium heat for 5 minutes, stirring frequently. Remove from heat and thoroughly mash the bananas. Add ¼ teacup of water, and put back on heat again. Cook very gently for 3 or 4 minutes, stirring all the time. Mix the sugar and the remainder of the water together, pour onto the bananas. Keep boiling fairly quickly for 15–20 minutes, stirring frequently to prevent sticking. The mixture should be quite thick by now; add the flavouring, then remove from heat, and pour the halva onto a dish. Decorate with the crushed cardamom seeds or grated nutmeg and the sliced nuts. The appearance of the halva can be improved by adding a little yellow colouring matter before removing from the heat. The superfluous butter-fat can be drained from the halva.

   Kela halva is served warm or cold.

INDIAN cooking

Pumpkin or Marrow Halva

Petha Halva

450g (1lb) of pumpkin or firm,
   mature marrow (weighed after
   peeling and extracting the seeds)
½ teacup milk
175g (6oz) brown sugar
1 tablespoon sultanas

1 dessertspoon desiccated coconut
1 tablespoon sliced almonds
50–75g (2–3oz) butter-fat
½ teaspoon crushed cardamom
   seeds or grated nutmeg

For 6 people

Grate the pumpkin or marrow. Pour the milk into a thick aluminium frying pan and bring to the boil. Add the grated pumpkin or marrow and boil quickly for 8–10 minutes, stirring and mashing all the time, at the end of which the mixture should be fairly dry. Add the brown sugar, which will make the mixture very 'loose'. Continue boiling quickly for another 7 or 8 minutes, then add the well-washed sultanas, desiccated coconut and the finely sliced almonds: mix well and add the butter-fat. Fry over medium heat for 5 or 7 minutes, when the halva should be perfectly dry and of attractive colour.

Pour onto a buttered dish, and decorate with crushed cardamom seeds or grated nutmeg.

This halva is also a traditional sweet dish, and is very nourishing.

Egg Halva

Anda Halva

4 large eggs
75–100g (3–4oz) set butter-fat
1 teacup milk
150g (5oz) sugar
1½ tablespoons sultanas

1 tablespoon sliced mixed nuts
1 tablespoon desiccated coconut
½–1 teaspoon crushed cardamom
*   seeds or grated nutmeg*

For 4 people
Beat the eggs for several minutes. Melt the butter-fat in an aluminium saucepan, and put in the egg mixture. Fry very slowly for 4–5 minutes, stirring all the time. Mix the milk and sugar together, and boil until the sugar is thoroughly dissolved, then pour this syrup over the simmering egg mixture. Add the well-washed and slightly soaked sultanas, and boil gently for about 10 minutes, stirring frequently. The halva by now should be fairly thick. Pour this on to a shallow dish, decorate with the sliced nuts, desiccated coconut and crushed cardamom seeds or grated nutmeg.

   This halva is nourishing and delicious to eat.

Sweet Vermicelli

Sweet Saivia (Sivaiya)

75g (3oz) sugar
1 tablespoon golden syrup
300ml (½ pint) water
1½ tablespoons set butter-fat

90g (3½oz) slightly broken
  vermicelli
1 teaspoon crushed cardamom seeds
  or grated nutmeg

For 5 people

Mix together the sugar, syrup and water, and boil for a few minutes. Put this by you in a jug. Heat the butter-fat, and gently fry the vermicelli in it until it is of a rich golden colour. Pour onto this the previously prepared syrup mixture, and boil quickly for 2–3 minutes. Turn the heat low, and gently boil until there is no superfluous moisture left in the vermicelli.

To prevent sticking, it is better to finish off cooking the vermicelli in a moderately hot oven.

When ready, the sweet vermicelli should be a golden brown colour, not mashy or sticking together. Mix in the crushed cardamom seeds or nutmeg after taking the vermicelli out of the oven, and serve piping hot.

Pancake

Malpura (Malpua)

*1 teacup fine wholemeal and
    plain flour mixed
3 tablespoons sugar
½ teaspoon baking powder*

*Just over ½ teacup of milk and water
1 teaspoon somph (aniseed), or a
    few drops lemon essence
2 or 3 tablespoons set butter-fat*

For 5 malpuras

Sieve the flour in a mixing bowl, add sugar and baking powder, and gradually add the warmed-up milk and water. The batter for malpuras should be of medium thickness. Beat for several minutes, add somph or lemon essence, and beat once again. Leave in a warm place for about an hour.

Melt 1 tablespoon of butter-fat in a frying pan, beat the batter once more, adding a tablespoon more of water if necessary; then pour two tablespoons of the batter into a teacup, and from the teacup spread it evenly on the smoking fat, taking care to keep the malpura as round as possible. Fry over medium heat, fairly quickly, and in plenty of fat. When light brown on both sides, remove from the pan and place in a shallow dish. Repeat the process until all the malpuras are fried.

When ready, the edges of the malpuras will be crisp, but the centre will be more like the usual pancake. They can be piled one on top of the other, and are usually served just warm. They are a great favourite during the rainy season, and in some places are served with rice pudding.

INDIAN cooking

Sweet Rice with Nuts and Sultanas

Mithe Chawal

1 teacup best rice
1 teacup sugar
2 teacups hot water
1 tablespoon set butter-fat

2 tablespoons sultanas
2 tablespoons finely sliced mixed nuts
1 teaspoon cardamom seeds or
    grated nutmeg

First method

For 4 people

Sort, wash and soak the rice for at least 10 minutes. Mix the sugar and water together, and keep this thin syrup in a jug. Heat the butter-fat in a heavy aluminium saucepan, and fry the well-drained rice in it very gently for a few minutes. Warm the syrup, and add this and the well-washed sultanas, together with the peeled and sliced nuts and the cardamom seeds (whole) or the nutmeg. Bring to the boil, then turn heat very low. At this stage it is better to put the saucepan (covered) in a pre-heated oven for 1 hour 15 minutes, on 180°C/350°F/Gas 4. When ready, the rice should be well cooked, but not broken or sticking together.

As its quality often varies, some rice may take a little less water in the syrup, and the cooking time may also be slightly varied. Many people mix a teaspoon of diluted saffron while the rice is cooking, to colour it and give it fragrance.

Second method

The ingredients are the same as in the previous recipe. The difference in the method being that after frying the rice in the butter-fat, you pour hot water on it instead of the syrup. Sultanas are added as before. Bring to the boil and turn the heat down very low. After 30 minutes, when rice should be quite tender and dry, add the sugar, skinned and sliced nuts, cardamom seeds or nutmeg. Stir with the end of the spoon, and cook very gently (covered) for 25 minutes or a little longer on the gas ring or in the oven.

Sweet rice is very good, and is usually served warm. The flavour of the rice is improved if it can be kept (covered) in a very low oven indeed for some minutes before serving.

Similar to Rice Pudding

Khir

1.5 litres (2½ pints) of milk
  (preferably full-fat milk)
65g (2½oz) rice
200g (7oz) sugar
1 tablespoon sultanas

2 dozen almonds
1 teaspoon crushed cardamom seeds
  or grated nutmeg
1 tablespoon rosewater

For 5 or 6 people

Pour the milk into a large, thick aluminium saucepan, and bring to the boil. Then add the well-washed rice, mix with a large spoon, and keep boiling on medium heat for an hour, stirring frequently and scraping from the sides and base to prevent sticking. Then add sugar, well-washed sultanas, blanched and thinly-sliced almonds, and the crushed cardamom seeds or grated nutmeg. At this stage, the khir may be put in a pre-heated moderate oven (190°C/375°F/Gas 5) for about 30 minutes to become brown on the top; but in India, after adding the sugar, sultanas, etc., we keep boiling gently until the right consistency is obtained. This does not take more than 15 minutes. Then the khir is transferred into a dish, and when slightly cold the rosewater is mixed into it.

Khir can be served warm or cold. If kept in a refrigerator overnight, it is even more delicious.

INDIAN cooking

Semolina Milk Pudding

Khir Suji

4 tablespoons semolina
1 tablespoon set butter-fat
900ml (1½ pints) milk
5 tablespoons sugar

2 tablespoons sultanas
1 teaspoon separated cardamon
    seeds or grated nutmeg

For 4 or 5 people
Using a heavy aluminium saucepan, fry the semolina gently in the butter-fat for about 7 minutes, stirring all the time. When the butter-fat separates from the semolina it is ready. Pour the milk on it and stir quickly; add the sugar and the well-washed sultanas. Keep stirring until the pudding thickens. Add the cardamom seeds or the nutmeg, cover the pudding and allow to simmer for 15–20 minutes, stirring occasionally. Instead of letting it simmer, the pudding can be transferred into a heatproof glass dish without the lid, and placed in a pre-heated oven at 200°C/400°F/Gas 6 for 20–30 minutes to brown.

This pudding is easily digested, and it is very tasty. It is usually served hot, though some people may prefer it cold.

Vermicelli Milk Pudding

Khir Saivia (Sivaiya)

1 dessertspoon set butter-fat
50g (2oz) slightly broken vermicelli
2½ teacups milk
3 tablespoons sugar

1 tablespoon well washed sultanas
½ teaspoon crushed cardamom
*   seeds or nutmeg*

For 4 people
Heat the butter-fat in a saucepan; add vermicelli and fry very gently until it becomes a golden brown colour, which should not take more than 7 minutes. Pour in the milk, bring to the boil and keep boiling over medium heat for 10 minutes. Add sugar and sultanas, and continue boiling (uncovered) for another 15 minutes, stirring frequently. When the desired consistency is obtained, it should be taken off the heat and poured into a glass heatproof or china dish, and decorated with the crushed cardamom seeds or grated nutmeg.

Khir saivia is usually served as an after-dinner sweet, either warm or cold.

Similar to Blancmange

Phirni

1.2 litres (2 pints) milk
2½ tablespoons cornflour, mixed
  in with a little milk
5 tablespoons sugar

1–2 dozen pistachio nuts or
  almonds, sliced
1 teaspoon crushed cardamom seeds
  or nutmeg

For 4 people
Place the milk in a large heavy aluminium saucepan and add the cornflour. Bring to the boil and keep boiling over medium heat for 15 minutes, stirring frequently. Add the sugar, and keep boiling for another 15–20 minutes. By now, the mixture should be fairly thick – though not as thick as the ordinary blancmange mixture. Mix in half of the nuts, pour the mixture into glass, heatproof dishes, decorate with nuts and crushed cardamom seeds or nutmeg and leave to cool.

When stirring, care should be taken not to scrape at the bottom or round the sides too much.

Store in a cool place, or in the refrigerator.

Condensed Milk Sweet

Rabri

900ml (1½ pints) fresh milk
  (preferably full-fat)
1½ tablespoons sugar

½ tablespoon separated (not crushed)
  cardamom seeds (optional)
1 dessertspoon rosewater

For 3 or 4 people
Using a deep heavy frying pan, bring the milk to the boil. Then turn the heat down low and boil gently, stirring frequently in the centre and keeping the cream and the skin of the milk to the sides. Do this for an hour and a quarter, until only about a quarter of the milk remains. Add the sugar and the cardamoms, and boil for a few minutes more. Eventually scrape all the cream and skin from the sides, and mix it all in. Remove from the heat, allow to cool, and add the rosewater.

    Rabri is always served cold. Some people add sliced pistachio nuts to it. It can be eaten as it is, or mixed with fresh fruit salad.

INDIAN cooking

Rice Dishes

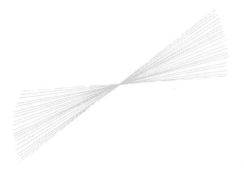

Savoury Rice

Namkin Chawal

1 teacup rice
1 dessertspoon set butter-fat

1 teaspoon salt
2 teacups hot water

For 3 or 4 people
Sort and wash the rice, and let it soak for at least 15 minutes. Heat the butter-fat in a thick aluminium saucepan, and place the well-drained rice into it. Add salt, and let it sizzle for a few minutes, stirring all the time; add the hot water, and bring quickly to the boil. Cover the saucepan well, and turn heat very low, then cook for 20–30 minutes without stirring. After the rice comes to the boil, it is better to pour it into a heatproof dish and cook it in a pre-heated low oven (150°C/300°F/Gas 2) for 30 minutes. When ready, the rice should be tender and perfectly dry.

This will go with any curried dish.

INDIAN cooking

Kedgeree made with Rice and Pulses

Khichri

1 teacup rice
5–6 teacups water
2½ teaspoons salt

1 teacup dal moong or red lentils
1 tablespoon set butter-fat
1½ teaspoons garam-masala

For 4 or 5 people

Sort, wash and soak the rice for a few minutes. Put the water on to boil in a large, heavy aluminium saucepan. Add the drained rice and salt, bring to the boil, and then turn heat down very low. Cook for 20 minutes, then add the well-washed and drained pulses. Mix slightly, and keep cooking (covered) over a very low heat for another 15 minutes. By now the rice and pulses should be quite tender, but not broken. If the rice is inclined to stick, place the saucepan (covered) in a pre-heated oven (170–180°C/325–350°F/Gas 3–4) to finish off the cooking. If, however, the khicharhi has too much fluid, let it remain on the heat (uncovered) with the heat slightly higher.

When cooked, the khichri should have the consistency of thick porridge, but the rice and pulses should not be crushed.

Heat the butter-fat in a small frying pan, add garam-masala and any other flavouring desired – onions, etc – and pour this onto the khichri. It can be kept hot in a very low oven (around 150°C/300°F/Gas 2) until the time of serving.

Instead of lentils and dal moong, whole moong and dal channa or yellow split peas can be mixed with the rice. The only difference in method is that these are added with the rice from the beginning, instead of in the middle of the cooking.

This khichri is easily digested and is often given to invalids and young children with or without the butter-fat and garam-masala.

Rice Pulao with Peas

Matar Pulao (Pulav)

1½ teacups best rice
1½ tablespoons butter-fat
5 cloves
2 small pieces cinnamon
½ teaspoon turmeric (optional)

1 teaspoon caraway seeds (optional)
1½ teaspoons salt
1½ teacups freshly shelled peas
2½ teacups hot water

For 6 people
Sort, wash and soak the rice for a half to one hour. Heat the butter-fat in a heavy aluminium saucepan, and add the cloves and the pieces of cinnamon, and, if desired, the turmeric and caraway seeds. Keep the heat very low, and fry these only for a minute or two. Then add the washed and drained rice, salt and peas. Mix and fry gently for a few minutes, stirring all the time. Next add the hot water. Mix thoroughly and bring to the boil quickly. Then turn the heat down very low and cook, either on the gas ring, or better still, in a pre-heated oven (180°C/350°F/Gas 4) for 30 minutes, with the lid on.

This pulao is very popular and delicious, and goes well with meat or vegetable dishes.

INDIAN cooking

Rice Pulao with Potatoes

Alu Pulao

With the obvious modification of using 225g (½lb) of potatoes, scraped and cut in small pieces, instead of peas, the ingredients and the method for this pulao are the same as for the previous recipe.

Rice Pulao with Cauliflower

Gobhi Pulao

In this pulao, medium-sized pieces of cauliflower are used instead of potatoes. The rest of the ingredients, and the method, remain the same as before, page 25.

Rice Pulao with Sultanas

Kishmish Pulao

In this, about 4 tablespoons of well-washed sultanas are used instead of vegetables. The rest of the ingredients, and the method, remain the same as before, page 25.

Rice Pulao with Spicy Lentil Cakes

Varia Pulao

In this pulao, 5 or 6 medium-sized varia (see page 95) are used instead of peas. But it is necessary to fry the varia with other spices before adding the rice. The rest of the ingredients, and the method, remain the same, page 25.

Rice Pulao with Chicken or Meat

Yakhni Pulao

For Meat

175g (6oz) chicken or meat
   (cut into quite small pieces)
3 teacups water

1 small onion, sliced
1 teaspoon salt

For Pulao

225g (8oz) rice
1 medium sized onion
1 tablespoon set butter-fat
½ teaspoon turmeric
½ teaspoon salt

4 cloves
1 teaspoon garam-masala
1 tablespoon milk-curd
½ teacup water

For 5 or 6 people

Using a saucepan, cook the meat gently in the 3 teacups of water, with onion and salt, for one hour, when the meat should be quite tender. Pour the stock into a jug, and keep that and the meat near at hand.

Sort, wash and soak the rice for 15 minutes. Using a heavy aluminium saucepan, fry the sliced onion gently in the butter-fat; add turmeric and ½ teaspoon salt, cloves and garam masala. Mix for a minute or two, then add the milk-curd and the pieces of meat. Fry gently for 7 minutes, then add the drained rice. Stir and fry for 2–3 minutes, then add 2 teacups of the meat stock and ½ teacup of water. If the stock is not enough, make it up by adding some more water. Stir and bring to boil, then turn the heat down very low. Cook very gently, either on the gas ring, or by placing the saucepan (covered) in a pre-heated oven (180°C/350°F/Gas 4). Yakhmi pulao is served hot with other meat or vegetable dishes, and is very tasty when eaten with milk curd.

Some people garnish the pulao with fried onions and hard-boiled eggs.

INDIAN cooking

Rice Pulao with Fish

Machchi Pulao I

1½ teacups best rice
350g (12oz) filleted cod (fresh or
    smoked), or similar fish
1½ tablespoons set butter-fat
1 teaspoon turmeric
2 or 3 small bunches fresh dhania
    (coriander) or parsley
3 or 4 dried red chillies, or ½
    teaspoon chilli powder (optional)

1–2 teaspoons garam-masala
1½–2 teaspoons salt
1 dessertspoon lemon juice
1 medium sized onion, peeled
    and chopped
2½ teacups hot water

For 5 or 6 people
Sort, wash and soak the rice for 15–20 minutes. Wash and dry the fish, then cut into pieces of the desired size. Heat half a tablespoon of butter-fat in a frying pan, add turmeric, chopped herbs, chillies, garam-masala, and ½ teaspoon of salt if smoked fish is being used, or 1 teaspoon of salt if fish is fresh. Let this sizzle for 2 or 3 minutes, then add the lemon juice. Dry the mixture by turning the heat up slightly higher, place the pieces of fish carefully in this sizzling pan, and fry them on both sides, mixing the fried herbs, etc., well into them. When they are cooked, not broken (which should not take more than 7 minutes), remove from the pan and place on a plate.

   Using a heavy aluminium saucepan, fry the onions gently in the remaining butter-fat. Add the remainder of the salt, and the well-washed rice; mix, and fry very slowly for 2 or 3 minutes. Mix in the fried herb mixture and the gravy left in the frying pan; mix thoroughly, and pour in the 2½ teacups of hot water. Bring to the boil, and turn heat very low; put a tight lid on, and keep over a low heat or in a low oven (150°C/300°F/Gas 2) for 30 minutes. After that, stir with the end of a wooden spoon, and place the fish pieces on top. Put the lid on again and keep over a very low heat for another 10–15 minutes. The pulao will then be ready to serve.

Rice Pulao with Prawns

Machchi Pulao II

The above dish can be prepared by using shelled and washed prawns instead of cod.

INDIAN cooking

Chicken and Meat

Chicken Curry

3 medium-sized onions, peeled
4 cloves garlic
A small piece of ginger and 1
   teaspoon chilli powder (optional)
1½ tablespoons set butter-fat
2 tablespoons broken-up fresh
coriander or sage

1½ teaspoons turmeric
1½ teaspoons garam-masala
3 teaspoons salt
4 large tomatoes, sliced
2 tablespoons stale milk curd
1.4kg (3lbs) young chicken(pieces)

For 8 people
Mince the onions, garlic and ginger (if using) together. Heat the butter-fat in a large saucepan and fry the onion mixture therein gently for a few minutes. Add the herbs, turmeric, garam-masala, salt and chilli powder (if using). Stir well and allow to sizzle for a little longer. Add well-washed pieces of chicken and fry for several minutes. Then cover it with a tight lid and cook gently for 1½ hours, adding a little hot water if too dry. After that, add the tomatoes and the curd. Stir well, and let the curry simmer for another 20 minutes. If there is too much gravy, the lid can be kept off for the last 20 minutes of cooking.

    When ready, the chicken curry can be kept hot, well covered, in a pre-heated low oven (150°C/300°F/Gas 2) for an hour or so. It is delicious with rice pulao and other vegetable dishes.

    Some chicken may take a longer time to get tender.

INDIAN cooking

Chicken Curry – Dry

Bhuna Chicken

1 medium-sized onion, peeled and
  chopped
3 cloves of garlic, peeled
A small piece of ginger
3 or 4 small bunches fresh chopped
  coriander, or other fresh herbs
1 teaspoon turmeric
2 teaspoons salt
1–2 teaspoons garam-masala

1 teaspoon chilli powder (optional)
1¼ tablespoons set butter-fat
3 medium-sized tomatoes
2 tablespoons milk-curd
700g (1½lb) tender chicken (cut into
  desired sized pieces)
1 dessertspoon desiccated coconut
1 dessertspoon lemon juice

For 4 or 5 people
Mince, or pound in a mortar, the onions, garlic, ginger and herbs. Mix in the
turmeric, salt, garam-masala and the chilli powder (if using). Using a large
heavy saucepan, fry this mixture slowly in the butter-fat for 3 or 4 minutes.
Add sliced tomatoes and the curd, and mix well. Reduce the superfluous
liquid by turning the heat up higher. Lastly, add the well-washed pieces of
chicken, stir and fry for 5 minutes. Then put a tight lid on, and turn the heat
down quite low. No liquid is required. Keep over the heat until the chicken
is really tender, which should not take more than 2 hours.

Mix well, and reduce any remaining gravy by turning heat up higher and
leaving the saucepan uncovered for a while. Add the desiccated coconut
and the lemon juice; let it simmer, uncovered, for another 5 minutes, when
the chicken should be ready to serve.

Any kind of poultry can by dry curried by this method.

Chicken Curry with Curd and Potatoes

Chicken Vindaloo

450g (1lb) potatoes (fairly small)
2 medium-sized onions, peeled
4 cloves garlic, peeled
2 tablespoons broken-up coriander
    or other fresh herbs
A small piece of ginger, and ½
    teaspoon chilli powder (optional)
3 teaspoons salt

1½ teaspoons garam-masala
½ teacup stale milk-curd or vinegar
900g (2lb) chicken (cut into small
    pieces, with only few bones left in)
1½ tablespoons set butterfat
1½ teaspoons turmeric
3 medium sized tomatoes
1½–2 teacups water

For 7 people

Scrub and boil the potatoes in their jackets (not too soft). When cool, skin and cut them in halves lengthwise, and place in a shallow dish. Mince the onions, garlic, herbs and ginger together; mix them with the salt, garam-masala, chilli powder and the stale curd or vinegar. Take half of this onion mixture and mix the potatoes and the well-washed pieces of chicken with it, and let stand for 1–2 hours. Using a large, heavy aluminium saucepan, fry the remainder of the onion mixture in the butter-fat. Add the turmeric, and soon after put in the sliced tomatoes, and fry gently for a little while longer. Add the seasoned pieces of chicken, mix thoroughly and fry for 5–10 minutes. Next add the 1½ teacups of warm water, bring to the boil, then turn the heat down low and cook with the lid on until the chicken is tender, which should not take more than 1½ hours. Add the seasoned potatoes, carefully mixing them in with the chicken. If necessary, add a little more hot water, and simmer on the gas ring or in a low oven (150°C/300°F/Gas 2) for 30 minutes.

Chicken vindaloo is very tasty with peas pulao and other vegetable dishes.

INDIAN cooking

Rabbit Curry

900g (2lb) jointed rabbit
2 medium-sized onions, peeled
4 cloves garlic, peeled
7g (¼oz) fresh or root ginger
1½ tablespoons set butter-fat
1 teaspoon turmeric
1½ teaspoons garam-masala

2–2½ teaspoons salt
1 teaspoon chilli powder (optional)
2 tablespoons fresh broken-up
  coriander or sage
3 medium-sized tomatoes
2 tablespoons milk-curd
1 dessertspoon lemon juice

For 4 or 5 people
Soak the rabbit pieces in cold, salted water for 30 minutes or longer. Wash them well and leave to drain. Chop finely or mince the onions, garlic and ginger, and gently fry this mixture in the butter-fat in a large, thick saucepan for 2 or 3 minutes. Add the turmeric, garam-masala, salt, chilli powder and chopped herbs; let these sizzle in the usual way. Add sliced tomatoes, and after frying them a little while, add in the milk-curd. Let the mixture reduce slightly, then add the pieces of rabbit; mix well, and fry uncovered for 5 minutes. After that, cover well and turn heat down low.

No liquid is required, because the natural juice from the rabbit will be sufficient to prevent burning, and to supply gravy. If, however, an extra juicy curry is required, then half a teacup of hot water should be added at this stage.

Cook the curry slowly, well covered, until the rabbit is tender; this will take 1½–2 hours. Lemon juice should be added 5 minutes before removing from heat.

Like many other curries, this one can be left in a preheated, very low oven (150°C/300°F/Gas 2) until ready to serve, and it can be re-heated.

Hare Curry can also be made by the above method.

Lamb or Mutton Curry

450g (1lb) meat
1 medium-sized onion, peeled
4 cloves garlic, peeled
7g (¼oz) ginger (fresh or root)
1 large red pepper or some
   fresh herbs
1 tablespoon set butter-fat

1 teaspoon turmeric
1 teaspoon garam-masala
2 teaspoons salt
½ teaspoon chilli powder (optional)
3 medium-sized tomatoes
1½ teacups hot water

For 4 or 5 people

Slice the meat into pieces of the desired size, removing excessive fat; wash it and keep it ready. Using a saucepan, fry the minced or chopped onions, garlic, ginger and the sweet peppers or herbs in the butter-fat. Add the turmeric, garam-masala, salt and chilli powder (if using); mix well and let it sizzle for a few minutes. Add the pieces of meat, and keep stirring for a little longer. Put the lid on and cook on low heat for 35 minutes, then add the sliced tomatoes. Let this fry for 2–3 minutes, add hot water, bring to the boil and turn the heat down low. Cook for another 35 minutes, when the meat should be quite tender. If there is too much gravy, the lid can be taken off for a few minutes and the heat turned up higher.

This curry can be kept hot in a very low pre-heated oven (150°C/300°F/Gas 2), or re-heated, as desired. It is delicious with rice pulaos.

Meat Cooked In Curd – Dry

Khorrma

450g (1lb) meat (with a little of
   the fat left in)
½ teacup milk-curd
1½ teaspoons salt
6 cloves of garlic, peeled
½ teaspoon chilli powder, and a
   small piece of ginger (optional)
1 tablespoon fresh coriander or
   other fresh herbs

1 medium-sized red pepper (optional)
1 medium-sized onion, peeled
1 dessertspoon set butter-fat
1 teaspoon turmeric
1 teaspoon garam-masala
1 dessertspoon desiccated coconut
2 medium-sized tomatoes

For 4 people
Wash and cut the meat into pieces of the desired size, soak in curd for 5
minutes, add one teaspoon of salt, then cook gently, mixed with the curd, in
a covered saucepan until it is tender and dry. This will take about one hour.
Remove from the heat.

   Mince the garlic, ginger (if using), herbs and red pepper together, then,
using another saucepan, fry this mixture gently with the sliced onions in the
butter-fat. Add turmeric, and the remainder of the salt, garam-masala, chilli
powder (if using) and the desiccated coconut. Fry for 2–3 minutes, then add
sliced tomatoes. Let them get tender, then add the already prepared meat.
Mix well, and simmer (uncovered) for 10–15 minutes.

   When ready, the khorrma should be quite dry and of an attractive colour.

Mutton Curry with Potatoes

450g (1lb) fairly lean mutton
   (cut into pieces)
1 medium-sized onion, peeled
2 cloves of garlic
1 red pepper (optional)
A small piece of ginger
1 tablespoon set butter-fat
1 heaped teaspoon turmeric
2 tablespoons broken-up coriander
   or other fresh herbs

2½ teaspoons salt
1–2 teaspoons garam-masala
½ teaspoon – or more – of chilli
   powder (optional)
1 tablespoon milk-curd
3 medium-sized tomatoes
225g (½lb) small potatoes
½ teacup hot water
1 dessertspoon lemon juice

For 3 or 4 people

Wash and drain the meat; scrape (don't peel) the potatoes. Fry the chopped or minced onions, garlic, red pepper and ginger in the butter-fat; add the turmeric, herbs, salt, garam-masala and the chilli powder (if using), and let this sizzle for 2 or 3 minutes. Add the milk-curd and thinly sliced tomatoes; stir well, and keep over medium heat (uncovered) for 4–5 minutes. Add the meat pieces, and allow to sizzle for another 5 minutes, then cover with a tight lid. Keep over a low heat for 35–40 minutes. Add the potatoes, and mix them well in. Pour in ½ teacup hot water. Let the curry bubble, then turn heat down low again. Keep the pan over the heat until the meat and potatoes are tender, and the desired amount of gravy is left. This should not take more than 30 minutes. Add the lemon juice about 5 minutes before removing from the heat. The curry improves if it is allowed to simmer longer, and it can be re-heated.

    This curry is a meal in itself, and goes well with rice pulao. Any other meat can be prepared by the above method.

Liver Curry

350g (12oz) liver
1 medium-sized onion, peeled
2 cloves of garlic, peeled
2 tablespoons broken-up fenugreek
   or other herbs
1 tablespoon set butter-fat

1 teaspoon turmeric
1½ teaspoons salt
½ teaspoon chilli powder (optional)
4 large tomatoes
1 teaspoon garam-masala
1 dessertspoon lemon juice

For 3 or 4 people

Wash and cut the liver into cubes of the desired size. Using a saucepan, fry the sliced onions, garlic and the herbs very gently in the butter-fat. Add the turmeric, salt and the chilli powder. Let this sizzle for 2–3 minutes, then add the liver. Mix and fry for another 5 minutes, then cover and cook very gently for 30 minutes. Add squares of tomatoes and cook for another 20–25 minutes. The liver should now be quite tender. Add garam-masala and lemon juice, and if there is too much gravy, uncover the saucepan and turn the gas up higher for a few minutes. Otherwise, simmer for 5 minutes and serve while it is hot.

   Rice pulao and vegetable dishes go very well with this curried liver.

Cold Cooked Meat Curry

225g (½lb) cold cooked meat
1 medium-sized onion, peeled
1–2 tablespoons fresh chopped
   fenugreek or any other fresh
   herbs
¾ tablespoon set butter-fat
½ teaspoon turmeric
½ teaspoon garam-masala

1 teaspoon salt
A pinch of chilli powder
1 dessertspoon finely desiccated
   coconut
3 medium-sized tomatoes
2 tablespoons milk-curd
1 teaspoon lemon juice (if desired)

(No water is required)

For 3 people

Carve the meat into pieces of the desired size, removing excessive fat. Mince, or very finely chop, the onions and herbs, and fry them gently in the butter-fat, as usual. Add turmeric, garam-masala, salt, chilli powder and the desiccated coconut; mix and fry for another 2–3 minutes. Then add the very thinly sliced tomatoes and the milk-curd. Let these simmer for 5 minutes, then add the meat; mix well, and cover with a tight lid. Turn the heat down low and keep it on for 10–15 minutes. Add the lemon juice (if using) just before taking the curry off the heat.

All kinds of cold meat, including cold chicken or other poultry, can be curried by this method, and the dish is easy to prepare.

INDIAN cooking

Minced Meat and Peas

Keema (Qima) I

350g (12oz) lean meat
1 medium-sized onion, peeled
1 tablespoon broken-up coriander
   or any other herbs
3 cloves garlic
A small piece of ginger, and ½
   teaspoon chilli powder (optional)

1 tablespoon set butter-fat
1 teaspoon turmeric
1½ teaspoons salt
4 medium-sized tomatoes
1 teacup freshly shelled peas
1 teaspoon garam-masala

For 4 people
Remove any fat from the meat, wash, dry and mince finely. Mince or chop finely the onion, herbs, garlic and ginger (if using). Use a saucepan, fry the onion mixture gently in the butter-fat; add the turmeric, salt and chilli powder (if using), and let this sizzle for a few minutes. Add the sliced tomatoes, mix well, and fry gently for 3 minutes. Add the minced meat, mix well; keep over a low heat for a few minutes, then cover with a tight lid and cook gently for 30 minutes, stirring occasionally. Add the well-washed peas, mix, and replace lid. Cook for another 20 minutes, add garam-masala and cook without a lid until all the excess liquid is reduced, and the meat is well fried. The skins of the tomatoes can be taken out with a spoon as they rise during cooking.

When ready, the keema should be a rich golden colour. It should be served hot with parathas (a variety of bread), and other vegetable curries.

Minced Meat and Bengal Split Peas

Keema (Qima) II

In this curry, ½ teacup of channa dal (split peas) is used instead of freshly shelled peas. Also, the split peas are added with the meat, and *not* after the meat has been cooked for 30 minutes. The rest of the ingredients, and the method, are the same as for the previous recipe.

INDIAN cooking

Meat Rolls in Potato Pastry

Meat Chaps

For Stuffing
1 medium-sized onion, peeled
A small piece of ginger, and ½
    teaspoon chilli powder (optional)
7g (¼oz) broken-up coriander or
    other fresh herbs
1 dessertspoon set butter-fat
½ teaspoon turmeric   lemon juice

1 teaspoon salt
2 medium-sized tomatoes
225g (½lb) lean meat (finely minced)
1½ teacups water
1 teaspoon garam-masala
1 dessertspoon ground mango or

For the Pastry, etc.
4 medium-sized potatoes
½ teaspoon salt
2 eggs

3 tablespoons breadcrumbs
600ml (1 pint) or more of oil or
    fat for frying

For 10 or 12 rolls
Using a saucepan, fry the finely chopped onions, ginger (if using) and the herbs gently in the butter-fat; add the turmeric, salt and chilli powder (if using), and fry gently for 2–3 minutes. Add the sliced tomatoes and let them get soft. Then add the minced meat and fry for 4–5 minutes over medium heat, stirring all the time, then pour on the water. Bring to the boil and turn heat down very low. Cook for 45 minutes, mix in the garam-masala and the ground mango or lemon juice. When ready, the meat should be tender and perfectly dry; mash it a little with a spoon, and let it cool.

Scrub the potatoes, and put them on to boil in their jackets. Remove them from the heat as soon as they feel tender (not mashy); when quite cold, skin them, add salt and crush and knead them for several minutes until they are as smooth as pastry. Beat the eggs and keep them by you; and place the breadcrumbs on a plate. Take a small piece of potato pastry, flatten it on your hand and place some of the meat mixture in the centre; then close it up so that the meat is inside the pastry. When all are fashioned, heat the oil or fat to smoking point in a deep-fat fryer or pan filled with oil or fat, dip each roll well in the egg mixture and roll in the breadcrumbs, then fry them two or three at a time in the fat.

When ready, meat rolls should be of golden-brown colour all round. They are delicious eaten with chutney and other Indian dishes.

Meat Balls

Koftas

1 medium-sized onion, peeled
  and chopped
1 medium-sized red pepper,
  chopped (optional)
2 tablespoons broken coriander or
  any other fresh herbs
6 cloves garlic, peeled and chopped

450g (1lb) finely minced lean meat
2 teaspoons salt
1 teaspoon garam-masala
½ teaspoon chilli powder (optional)
1 large egg
Some oil or fat for frying

For 6 people
Mince the onions, red peppers (if using), herbs and garlic together, then mix these in the minced meat. Add salt, garam-masala and chilli powder (if using). Knead this mixture until it is a stiff smooth dough. Divide into walnut-sized balls, dip into the well-beaten egg and fry slowly in the deep, hot fat.

Koftas can be served as they are at tea time with some fresh mint chutney, or they can be curried in the following way:

1 medium-sized onion, peeled
A little chopped ginger and chilli
  powder (optional)
1 tablespoon set butter-fat
1 teaspoon turmeric
1 teaspoon salt

½ teaspoon garam-masala
225g (½lb) tomatoes
1 tablespoon stale milk-curd or
  lemon juice
1 teacup hot water

Using a saucepan, fry the minced or chopped onions and ginger (if using) in the butter-fat; add the turmeric, salt, garam-masala and chilli powder (if using). Allow to sizzle for a few minutes, then add sliced tomatoes and the curd. Fry well, then put in the koftas. After stirring for 5 minutes, pour in the hot water. Let the curry simmer for 15 minutes, and then it should be ready to serve with savoury rice and other vegetable dishes.

Chicken Koftas can be made by the same method. Cold cooked meat can also be used instead of fresh meat.

Meat Balls with Eggs Inside

Nargisi Koftas

For Koftas

1 teacup water
450g (1lb) lean meat, finely minced
1 small onion, peeled
4 cloves garlic, peeled
1 teaspoon salt
½ teaspoon turmeric
1 teaspoon garam-masala

½ teaspoon chilli powder (optional)
1½ tablespoons besan or split-pea
  flour
7 eggs
1 tablespoon milk-curd
Some oil or fat for frying

For Curry

1 tablespoon (or more) set butter-fat
1 medium-sized onion, peeled
A small piece of ginger and ½
  teaspoon chilli powder (optional)
1 medium-sized red pepper
  deseeded and chopped, or 2
  tablespoons broken-up coriander
  or other herbs

1 teaspoon turmeric
1–1½ teaspoons salt
½–1 teaspoon garam-masala
2 large tomatoes
½ teacup milk-curd or milk
1 teacup hot water

To prepare meat for Koftas
For 6 people
Heat the water in a saucepan and add the finely minced meat. Add chopped onions and garlic, salt, turmeric, garam-masala and chilli powder (if using). Bring to the boil, then turn the heat down low and simmer for 30 minutes; add the flour, and cook for another 15 minutes. When the meat is very soft and dry, mash and knead as much as possible.

Beat one of the eggs in a bowl and keep it by you. Mix the tablespoon of milk-curd and a little of the beaten egg in with the meat, and knead once again. Hard-boil the remaining eggs, cool and peel them.

To shape the Koftas
Take some of the well-worked meat mixture, flatten it on your hand, and place one of the hard-boiled eggs inside it. Wrap the mixture round the egg,

using some more if necessary. Shape the rest of the koftas the same way.

Using a deep-fat fryer or deep chip-pan, heat the oil or fat to nearly smoking point. Dip each kofta in the beaten egg, then fry over medium heat until golden brown both sides. Drain well and place in a shallow dish.

To curry the Koftas
Using a large saucepan, fry gently in the butter-fat the minced or chopped onions, ginger (if using) and the red peppers or the herbs, for 2 or 3 minutes. Add turmeric, salt, chilli powder (if using) and garam-masala, then add the sliced tomatoes. Mix and simmer for a little while, then add the milk-curd and the hot water. Boil gently for 3–4 minutes, then add the koftas. Let these simmer for 2 or 3 minutes, then remove from the heat. Carefully cut each kofta in half and pour some gravy over it before serving.

Nargisi koftas are very tasty and are served hot at lunch or dinner time.

Meat Roasted on Skewers

Seek Kababs

275g (10oz) meat (with a little fat)
1 medium-sized onion, peeled
A small piece of ginger and ½
   teaspoon chilli powder (optional)
2 tablespoons broken-up coriander
   or other fresh herbs
1½ teaspoons salt

1 teaspoon garam-masala
1 dessertspoon ground mango or
   lemon juice
1 tablespoon fine besan or split-pea
   flour
2 tablespoons milk-curd
6 small metal meat skewers

For 4 people
Wash, cut and finely mince the meat. Mince the onion, ginger (if using) and herbs, and then mix these with the minced meat, together with the salt, garam-masala, chilli powder (optional), ground mango and the split-pea flour. Mix and knead for several minutes. It is better to place the mixture on a board and roll it down until it becomes like a smooth dough. Wrap a small portion of the mixture around one of the skewers in a small sausage shape. Paste it generously with the milk-curd. Place as many as convenient on a toasting grid under the hot grill, and keep turning them whilst roasting. When they are well-roasted on all sides, take them off the skewers and serve hot at dinner time, with fresh mint chutney and other curried dishes.

Note: Ground mango (amchoor) can be obtained from Indian grocery stores.

Meat Rissoles

Shami Kababs

1 medium-sized onion, peeled
A small piece of ginger
6 flakes of garlic
2 fresh green chillies, or a little chilli
   powder, if desired
7g (¼oz) fresh coriander or other
   fresh herbs
1 dessertspoon set butter-fat
½ teaspoon turmeric

1½ teaspoons salt
2 medium-sized tomatoes
350g (12oz) finely minced lean meat
1 tablespoon channa dal or split peas
1 teacup warm water
1 teaspoon or more of garam-masala
1 dessertspoon ground mango or
   lemon juice

For batter, etc.

2 tablespoons besan or split-pea
   flour
2 tablespoons or a little more of
   milk-curd or milk, for mixing

Salt
Some oil or fat for frying

For 10 Kababs

Using a saucepan, fry the minced onion, ginger, garlic, chillies and the herbs gently in the butter-fat. Add turmeric and salt, and afterwards add sliced tomatoes. Let this mixture sizzle for a few minutes, then add the well-washed, finely minced meat, and the split peas, washed and slightly soaked. Let these fry gently for 4–5 minutes, then add the water. Bring to the boil and turn the heat down low, and cook for nearly 45 minutes. Add garam-masala and the lemon juice. Mix, mash and dry the meat well. Let it cool, and mash thoroughly again, and shape into rissoles of the desired size.

Make the batter ready by mixing the split-pea flour with the milk-curd. Add a pinch of salt and beat until smooth. Heat the oil or fat (not deep fat) in a frying pan, and fry the kababs over medium heat, after coating each one well in the batter.

When ready, the kababs should be crisp and brown all round. Served at dinner time, they are delicious with chutney, or a piece of lemon which can be squeezed onto them to improve the flavour.

INDIAN cooking

Egg and Fish Recipes

Egg Curry

8 eggs
2 medium-sized onions, peeled
2 tablespoons broken up coriander
  or other fresh herbs
1½ tablespoons set butter-fat
1 teaspoon turmeric

2½ teaspoons salt
2 teaspoons desiccated coconut
½ teaspoon chilli powder (optional)
1 teaspoon garam-masala
4 medium-sized tomatoes
2 tablespoons milk-curd

For 4 people

Boil the eggs for ten minutes, shell and cut in halves lengthwise. Mince or finely chop the onions and herbs. Heat the butter-fat in a saucepan, and fry the onion mixture slowly. Add turmeric, salt, desiccated coconut, chilli powder (if using) and garam-masala. Mix well and allow to sizzle for two or three minutes. Add sliced tomatoes, stir well, then add the milk-curd. Fry gently, and lastly place the eggs carefully into the saucepan so that the yolks do not separate from the whites. With a spoon, cover the eggs with the gravy from the tomatoes and curd, put the lid on and allow the curry to simmer for ten minutes. Place in a vegetable dish, and serve hot with rice pulao or any other vegetable dish.

INDIAN cooking

Egg and Mushroom Curry

6 new laid eggs
225g (½lb) small white mushrooms
1 medium-sized onion, peeled
7g (¼oz) ginger
1 tablespoon set butter-fat
½ teaspoon turmeric
2 tablespoons fresh broken-up
    coriander, or other herbs

1–2 teaspoons garam-masala
½ teaspoon chilli powder (optional)
3 medium-sized tomatoes
1-2 tablespoons milk-curd
1 dessertspoon lemon juice
2 teaspoons salt

For 3 or 4 people
Hard-boil the eggs, shell them and cut them in half, slantwise. Soak and wash the mushrooms well under running water, and drain them. Fry the chopped onion and ginger gently in the butter-fat; add turmeric, chopped herbs, garam-masala and the chilli powder. Let these sizzle in the usual way, then add sliced tomatoes, the milk-curd and salt. Reduce excess liquid by turning the heat up slightly higher. Add the well-washed mushrooms, mix and fry for a little while, then cover the saucepan and cook over medium heat for 15 minutes. After that carefully place the eggs in the curry, and shake the saucepan so that the eggs get well mixed in the gravy. Cook, uncovered, for 15–20 minutes (if extra juicy curry is required, the lid should be kept on), shaking the pan frequently. Add lemon juice, mix well and the curry will be ready to serve. It goes very well with rice pulao or any of the breads.

Eggs and Peas

This curry can be prepared by using 1½ teacups of shelled garden peas, or well rinsed out frozen peas, instead of mushrooms. Otherwise, use the rest of the ingredients and follow the method as for the previous curry.

Eggs and Aubergine Curry

In this curry, 225g (½lb) of aubergines (cut into medium-sized pieces) are used instead of mushrooms.

Fish Curry

Machchi Curry

1 medium-sized onion, peeled
2 small cloves garlic, peeled
  (optional)
2 tablespoons broken-up coriander
  or parsley
1¼ tablespoons set butter-fat
1 teaspoon turmeric
1½ teaspoons salt

1 dessertspoon desiccated coconut
1 teaspoon garam-masala
½ teaspoon chilli powder (optional)
2 medium-sized tomatoes
2 tablespoons milk-curd or 1
  tablespoon lemon juice
450g (1lb) filleted cod or other
  fleshy filleted fish

For 4 people
Using a saucepan, fry the minced or finely chopped onion, garlic (if using) and herbs gently in the butter-fat. Add turmeric, salt, coconut, garam-masala and the chilli powder (if using). Mix well and allow to sizzle for a few minutes. Add sliced tomatoes and fry gently until they are tender. Crush the tomatoes in the gravy, then add the milk-curd (it should have been kept a day or two) or the lemon juice. Let the mixture cook over a medium heat for 4–5 minutes, then add the well-washed and drained fish, cut into desired pieces (not small), keeping the skin on. Mix very carefully and cover the fish with the gravy. When it starts to boil cover it and let the curry simmer for 7–10 minutes. The fish must not be allowed to become too soft and mashy. If less gravy is required, uncover the fish while it is simmering.

   This curry is very tasty with a dish of rice and pea pulao.

INDIAN cooking

Prawn and Potato Curry

600ml (1 pint) glass of fresh prawns
225g (½lb) small new potatoes
1 medium-sized onion, peeled
3 or 4 bunches of fresh chopped
    coriander or parsley
1 tablespoon set butter-fat
½ teaspoon turmeric

1 teaspoon salt
1 teaspoon garam-masala
½ teaspoon chilli powder (optional)
3 medium-sized tomatoes
½–1 teacup hot water
1 teaspoon lemon juice

For 3 people

Shell the prawns and wash them well. Scrape and wash the potatoes. Fry the chopped onions and herbs in the butter-fat; add turmeric, salt, garam-masala and the chilli powder. Let these sizzle for 2–3 minutes. Add sliced tomatoes, and finally the potatoes; mix and fry for a little while, then add the hot water. Bring to the boil and turn the heat down low, and cook for 15–20 minutes.

The potatoes by now should be quite tender, but not broken. Carefully mix in the washed prawns and the lemon juice. Let the curry simmer (covered) for 10 minutes and then it should be ready to serve.

This curry goes well with rice pulao and bread varieties.

Indian Fried Fish

Tali Machchi

400g (14oz) filleted plaice or
    lemon sole
2 teaspoons salt
1 teaspoon garam-masala
1 dessertspoon vinegar
2 tablespoons besan or split-pea
    flour

2 tablespoons plain flour
½ teacup warm water
2 tablespoons broken-up coriander or
    chopped parsley
½ teaspoon chilli powder (optional)
Some oil or fat for frying

For 5–6 persons

Remove any stray bones from the fillets, cut each one in half, and after washing them place them on a large plate and sprinkle on them 1 teaspoon of salt, ½ teaspoon garam-masala and the vinegar. Mix the besan and the plain flour together, and make into a thick batter by gradually adding the water. Add the rest of the salt and garam-masala, the herbs and the chilli powder (if using), and beat for several minutes. Put the oil or fat in a deep frying pan, and when it is smoking hot, place two or three pieces at a time of the fillets of fish in the pan, which have previously been well coated on both sides with the thick batter. The frying should be done fairly quickly to prevent the fish becoming saturated with the fat. When golden-brown on both sides, drain the pieces of fillet and place them on a greaseproof paper before arranging them on a large, shallow dish for serving.

This dish is very tasty with lemon pickle and curried potatoes and tomatoes.

INDIAN cooking

Stuffed Fish Rolls

450g (1lb) filleted plaice or lemon sole	2 tablespoons chopped coriander or parsley
2 teaspoons salt	2–3 small green chillis or ½ teaspoon chilli powder
6–7 tablespoons bread-crumbs	2 eggs, beaten
½ teacup milk	Some oil or fat for frying
1 large lemon for juice	
1 teaspoon garam-masala	
2 small, peeled and finely chopped onions	

For 5 or 6 people

Remove any stray bones from the fillets, wash and sprinkle a little salt on them.

To prepare the stuffing, mix 4 tablespoons of the bread-crumbs and milk together. Add a little of the lemon juice, the remainder of the salt, garam-masala, chopped onions, coriander or parsley, and chillis. Add a little of the beaten egg and mix thoroughly.

To stuff the fish, place one of the washed and salted fillets on a board, sprinkle some lemon juice over it and place about 2 tablespoons of stuffing on one half of the fillet, carefully folding the other half on top. Sprinkle a little more lemon juice on top, and coat with beaten egg, sticking the sides together as best you can. Roll it in breadcrumbs and fry in shallow hot fat until it is crisp and golden-brown on both sides. Drain and remove from the heat. Stuff and fry the rest of the fillets likewise.

These stuffed fish-rolls are very tasty and go well with tomato and potato curry.

Fish Balls

Fish Koftas

575g (1¼lb) fresh filleted cod
1 small onion, peeled
3–4 small bunches of coriander or
    parsley
1½ teaspoons salt
1 teaspoon garam-masala

½ teaspoon chilli powder (optional)
1 tablespoon ground mango
    (optional)
Some oil or fat for frying
2 eggs
2 tablespoons breadcrumbs

For 4 people
Bring the fish to the boil in water, take off the heat immediately, drain, and, when cool, remove the skin and any stray bones. Place in a mixing bowl and mash thoroughly. Add minced onions and herbs (squeezed dry), salt, garam-masala, chilli-powder (if using) and the ground mango. Mix well and shape the mixture into 12 balls. Heat the oil to boiling point and after dipping the koftas in the well beaten eggs and rolling them in the bread-crumbs, fry them in deep oil or fat over medium heat. These koftas are usually served hot, with tamarind chutney or any other relish.

INDIAN cooking

Stuffed Fish Rolls in Potato Pastry

450g (1lb) filleted fish
1 small, peeled and finely chopped onion
2 tablespoons coriander or parsley
1½ teaspoons salt
1 teaspoon garam-masala
½ teaspoon chilli powder (optional)

1 dessertspoon ground mango or lemon juice
450g (1lb) potatoes
2 eggs
2 tablespoons fine breadcrumbs
Some oil or fat for frying

For 12 rolls

Wash and steam the fish (not too soft), when cool and well drained, break into small pieces, skinning and boning where necessary. Place in a mixing bowl and add the onion, coriander or parsley, 1½ teaspoons salt, garam-masala, chilli powder (if using) and the ground mango or lemon juice. Mix well, and if it feels too moist, dry it by heating in a frying pan for a few minutes.

Boil the potatoes in their jackets, (ordinary mashed potatoes are not suitable), until they are cooked through, but not over-cooked. Skin them, and mash and knead them hard, using the palms of your hands. Add half teaspoon of salt. Beat the egg and keep it by you; also the breadcrumbs on a plate.

Flatten out a little of the potato pastry on the palm of your hand, place nearly 2 tablespoons of the fish mixture in the centre, then fold the edges in and fashion into a roll. When all the rolls are ready, dip each one into the beaten egg and then roll in the breadcrumbs.

Deep-fry two or three together over a medium heat until they are an appetizing golden-brown colour, and serve as soon as they are ready.

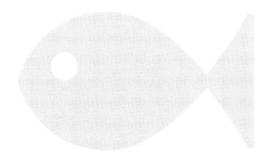

INDIAN cooking

Vegetable Dishes

Peas and Potatoes with Juice

1–1¼ tablespoons set butter-fat
2 medium-sized onions, peeled
2 tablespoons broken coriander
    or other fresh herbs
A small piece of fresh ginger and
    1 teaspoon chilli powder
    (optional)
1½ teaspoons turmeric

1¼ teaspoons garam-masala
2–3 teaspoons salt
3 tomatoes
350g (¾lb) potatoes, preferably
    small
1–2 teacups hot water
2 teacups shelled peas
1 tablespoon lemon juice

For 5 or 6 people
Heat the butter-fat in a large saucepan; add minced or chopped onions, herbs and ginger (if using), and fry gently for 4–5 minutes. Add turmeric, garam-masala, salt and chilli powder (if using); mix well and then add sliced tomatoes and potatoes which should be scraped and, if large, cut into halves or quarters. Let this sizzle for 10 minutes, stirring frequently. Add the peas, and after a few minutes pour in the hot water. Boil quickly at first, and then turn the heat down low. Cook until the peas and potatoes are tender (not broken) and then add the lemon juice. Simmer for another ten minutes – the skin of the tomatoes usually floats to the top and can be removed with a spoon. If there is too much gravy, it can be reduced by removing the lid and turning the heat up high for a while.

Most people like this curry and children simply love it. It can be served with a meat dish and plain savoury rice. Frozen or tinned peas can be used, but they should be well rinsed.

INDIAN cooking

Potato Curry – Dry

Sukhe Alu

450g (1lb) small potatoes
1 medium-sized onion, peeled
2 tablespoons broken-up
  coriander or any other fresh
  herbs
1 tablespoon set butter-fat

1 teaspoon turmeric
1½ teaspoons salt
½ teaspoon chilli powder
  (optional)
1 teaspoon garam-masala
1 tablespoon lemon juice

For 3 or 4 people
Scrape the potatoes and, if large, cut into halves and quarters. Using a
saucepan, fry the chopped onion and herbs gently in the butter-fat. Add the
turmeric, salt and chilli powder (if using). Mix well and then add the
potatoes. Stir for a few minutes, and then turn the heat low. Cook for 30
minutes with a tight lid on. If they are inclined to stick, sprinkle a little hot
water over them. It is better to place them (covered) in a pre-heated oven
(190°C/375°F/Gas 5) for those 30 minutes, if possible. Add the garam-
masala and lemon juice about 10 minutes before removing from heat.

New potatoes are particularly tasty when prepared in this way.

Potatoes and Dried Spicy Lentil Cakes

Alu and Varia (Baria)

1 medium-sized onion, peeled
Some chopped coriander or
    other herbs
½ teaspoon chilli powder
    and a piece of ginger
    (optional)
3 or 4 varia (see page 95)
1 tablespoon set butter-fat
1 teaspoon turmeric

1½ teaspoons salt
450g (1lb) potatoes
    (preferably small)
1 teacup hot water
3 medium-sized tomatoes
½ teaspoon garam-masala
½ teacup milk-curd or
    1 dessertspoon lemon juice

For 4 or 5 people.
Using a saucepan, fry the sliced onion, herbs, ginger (if using) and varia (if large, they should be broken into two or more pieces) gently in the butter-fat for a few minutes. The varia and onion should not be allowed to get too brown. Add the turmeric, salt and the chilli powder (if using), mix and fry for a minute or two, then add the potatoes (cut into halves or quarters). Stir and simmer for a while: add the hot water and bring to the boil, then turn the heat down low and cook for 15–20 minutes. The potatoes and varia should now feel tender, but not broken. Add the sliced tomatoes, garam-masala and the milk-curd or lemon juice. Let the curry simmer for 10–15 minutes.

This curry is delicious with rice pulao or any meat preparation.

INDIAN cooking

Potatoes and Fenugreek or Spinach

Alu and Methi

1 small piece fresh ginger or
   medium-sized onion, peeled
1 tablespoon set butter-fat
1 teaspoon turmeric
2 teaspoons salt
½ teaspoon chilli powder
   (optional)

700g (1½lb) potatoes
   (preferably small)
225g (½lb) fenugreek or
   spinach
1 teaspoon garam-masala

For 4 people

Fry the finely-sliced ginger or onion slowly in the butter-fat for a few minutes. Add the turmeric, salt and chilli powder (if using), and mix well. Add the potatoes – which should be scraped (not peeled) and cut into halves and quarters, if large – and allow to sizzle for a few minutes. Cover the frying pan and cook gently until the potatoes are slightly tender, which should take about 15 minutes.

Wash the fenugreek or spinach well, and cut quite small (the tender stalks should also be included); drain and add this to the frying potatoes. Mix well and cook for another 15 minutes without the lid. When the vegetables are tender and all the excess liquid has reduced, mix in the garam-masala.

Transfer the alu methi into a vegetable dish, cover it well and keep it in a pre-heated low oven (150°C/300°F/Gas 2) until ready to serve.

Potatoes and Tomatoes

Alu and Tamatar

2 medium-sized onions, peeled
15g (½oz) fresh ginger (optional)
1½ tablespoons set butter-fat
1 teaspoon turmeric
1 teaspoon garam-masala
2½ teaspoons salt
15g (½oz) fresh coriander or
    parsley

½ teaspoon chilli powder
    (optional)
700g (1½lb) potatoes
    (preferably small and
    round)
5 medium-sized tomatoes
1 teacup hot water

For 4 or 5 people

Slice and fry the onions and ginger (if using) in the butter-fat in the usual way; add the turmeric, garam-masala, salt, coriander or parsley and chilli powder (if using), and mix well. If the potatoes are large, cut into fair-sized pieces. Put these and the sliced tomatoes in the pan, and allow to sizzle for ten minutes. Add hot water, bring to the boil, cover and cook gently until the potatoes are tender, but not broken. The skins of the tomatoes may be removed as they float to the top.

Curried potatoes and tomatoes will go well with any other curried dish, meat or otherwise.

INDIAN cooking

Savoury Potato Balls

Alu Koftas

450g (1lb) good medium-sized
   potatoes
1½ teaspoons salt
1 teaspoon garam-masala
½ teaspoon chilli powder
   (optional)

1–2 tablespoons finely
   chopped coriander or
   other herbs
1 egg
Some oil or fat for frying

For 16 balls
Boil the potatoes in their jackets, (ordinary mashed potatoes will not do), and when the skin is just beginning to split, remove them from heat and out of the water. Allow to cool, then skin carefully, and crush and knead until they are like a smooth pastry. Mix the salt, garam-masala, chilli powder (if using) and the finely chopped herbs, and knead once again. Beat the egg and keep it by you. Heat the oil or fat in a deep-fat fryer or deep pan. Take a little of the potato pastry, shape it into a ball, and after quickly coating it with the egg mixture, fry it in the deep, hot fat over medium heat until it becomes a golden brown colour all round. Three or four koftas can be fried at a time.

    Alu koftas can be served hot at lunch or tea time. They are quite tasty eaten cold, particularly with salad.

Vegetable Dishes

Potato Cutlets Stuffed with Peas

Potato Chaps

4 medium-sized potatoes
1½ teaspoons salt
1 dessertspoon set butter-fat
2 small onions, peeled
A small piece of ginger and
   ½ teaspoon chilli powder
   (optional)
1–2 tablespoons chopped coriander
   or other herbs

½ teaspoon turmeric
1½–2 teacups tender peas
1 dessertspoon lemon juice
1 teaspoon garam-masala
2 eggs
About 3 tablespoons breadcrumbs
600ml (1 pint) of oil or its equivalent,
   for frying

For 10 Chaps
Boil the potatoes in their jackets; then skin, mash and knead them for several minutes. Add ½ teaspoon of salt to them. The mixture should be as smooth as pastry.

To prepare the stuffing
Using a saucepan, heat the butter-fat and very gently fry in it the chopped onions, ginger (if using) and herbs; add turmeric, chilli powder (if using) and the rest of the salt. After a minute or two, put in the well-washed peas; mix well, and sprinkle a little water over them, cover the saucepan and let them simmer until tender. Mix in the lemon juice and garam-masala before removing from the heat, which should be when they are well cooked and perfectly dry. Allow to cool slightly.

   Beat the eggs, and keep them and the breadcrumbs near at hand.

To shape the Chaps
Break off a piece of the potato pastry, flatten it in your hands, and place about a tablespoon of the peas mixture in the centre. Fold the edges together, so that you have the peas inside the potato mixture. Shape the chaps into some resemblance to meat chops, taking care not to flatten them too much, in case you uncover the peas. When all the chaps are prepared, coat each one thoroughly with the egg mixture, roll in the breadcrumbs, and fry in deep, hot fat over medium heat, until fairly brown on both sides.

   Potato chaps are very tasty eaten with tamarind or other chutneys. They are usually served hot at either lunch or tea time.

Potato and Aubergine Curry (Dry)

1–1½ teaspoons set butter-fat
4 small onions, peeled
A small piece of ginger, and
   1 teaspoon chilli powder
   (optional)
1½ teaspoons turmeric

1 teaspoon garam-masala
2 teaspoons salt
2 medium-sized tomatoes
6 small potatoes
4 medium-sized aubergines,
   unpeeled
1 dessertspoon lemon juice

For 5 or 6 people
Heat the butter-fat in a large deep frying pan, and fry gently the sliced onions and ginger (if using) for a few minutes. Add turmeric, garam-masala, salt and the chilli powder (if using). Mix well and allow to sizzle for a few minutes, then add sliced tomatoes. Fry quickly and reduce all the excess juice. Add scraped and washed potatoes. If these are large, cut them into halves or quarters. Mix well, and then add the aubergines (cut into pieces as desired – they must not be too small). If green and tender, the caps of the aubergines can be left on. Mix well and cook the curry over medium heat (uncovered) until the vegetables are tender (not broken), stirring them frequently with tongs or a fish slice to prevent them crushing. If however, the aubergines are rather tough, then, during the course of the cooking the curry should be covered for a time. Mix in the lemon juice before removing from heat; and when ready the curry should be quite dry and of an attractive colour.

   A dish of lentils or meat curry will go very well with it.

Curried Peas (Dry)

1 medium-sized onion, peeled
1½ tablespoons broken-up
   coriander or other herb
15g (½oz) ginger (fresh or root)
1 tablespoon set butter-fat
1 teaspoon turmeric

1–1½ teaspoons salt
½ teaspoon chilli powder (optional)
2 teacups fresh peas
1 teaspoon garam-masala
1 tablespoon lemon juice

For 4 people
Using a heavy saucepan, fry the chopped onions, herbs and ginger gently in the butter-fat. Add turmeric, salt and chilli powder (if using), and allow to sizzle for a few minutes. Add the well-washed and drained peas, mix thoroughly and cover the curry with a tight lid. Cook gently until the peas are tender; this should not take more than 20 minutes. About five minutes before removing from the heat, add the garam-masala and lemon juice. Any excess liquid may be reduced by removing the lid and turning the gas higher. Some people add a tiny piece of asafoetida (crushed and fried with the onions) to this curry.

Shelled broad beans can also be curried by the above method.

INDIAN cooking

Peas and Panir

For Panir
2 tablespoons tepid lemon juice or
    1 teacup tepid milk-curd

1.2 litres (2 pints) milk
Some oil or fat for frying the cubes

For the Curry, etc.
1¼ tablespoons set butter-fat
1 medium-sized onion, peeled
15g (½oz) coriander or other herb
7g (¼oz) ginger (fresh or root)
1 teaspoon turmeric
1 teaspoon garam-masala

1½ teaspoons salt
½ teaspoon chilli powder (optional)
2 teacups freshly shelled peas
4 small tomatoes
1 teacup butter milk from the panir
1 teaspoon lemon juice

For 3 or 4 people
To make the panir (soft milk cheese), add the lemon juice or milk-curd to 1.2
litres (two pints) of boiling milk, straining through a muslin bag and press
with fairly heavy pressure to drain out all the whey or butter-milk, which
should be kept in a jug. Place the panir on a board, and after rolling it out
thickly, carefully cut into small cubes. Fry these cubes very gently in shallow
fat or oil until they are of a golden-brown colour.

Using a saucepan, fry gently in the butter-fat the chopped onions, herbs
and ginger. Add turmeric, garam-masala, salt and chilli powder (if using),
and let these sizzle for a few minutes. Add the well-washed peas, mix and
cook gently with the lid on for 15 minutes. Then add the sliced tomatoes and
the cubes of panir, stirring and frying for 3–4 minutes. Next add the whey
(butter-milk) from the panir, bring to the boil, then turn the heat down quite
low and allow to simmer for 15–20 minutes. Add the lemon juice 10 minutes
before removing from heat.

Peas and Carrots

6 spring onions, peeled
2 tablespoons broken-up coriander
  or other herbs
1 dessertspoon set butter-fat
1 teaspoon turmeric
¾ teaspoon garam-masala
1½ teaspoons salt

2 fresh green chillies, or
  ½ teaspoon chilli powder
  (optional)
225g (½lb) carrots
1½ teacups freshly shelled peas
1 dessertspoon lemon juice

For 3 or 4 people

Using a saucepan, fry the sliced onions and herbs in the butter-fat. Add turmeric, garam-masala, salt and green chillis or chilli powder (if using). Add the scraped and washed carrots in small pieces; fry gently for a few minutes, then cover the saucepan and cook for another 15 minutes, then add the well-washed peas. Mix well, cover and keep cooking gently until the peas and carrots are tender and dry. Add lemon juice a few minutes before removing from the heat and serve hot with other curried dishes.

INDIAN cooking

Pea Pods Curried

The pods from 450g (1lb) of
    young peas
3 medium-sized potatoes
4 small spring onions, or 1
    medium-sized onion, peeled
A small piece of ginger (optional)

1 dessertspoon set butter-fat
1 teaspoon turmeric
1–1½ teaspoons salt
½ teaspoon chilli powder (optional)
1 large tomato
½ teaspoon garam-masala

For 3 people

After shelling the peas in the usual manner by popping the pod open lengthwise, divide the opposite side or the empty pod also, so that you have two 'leaves'. Holding one leaf, stalk upwards, with the inside towards you, bend the stalk end inwards about 1cm (½in) down until it cracks without completely breaking. Then, by gently pulling down, you can peel off the inner lining, often in one piece, which can be thrown away. Wash these soft outer 'leaves' of the pods, removing any stringy parts, cut them in halves, quarters or keep whole, as desired. Scrape, wash and cut the potatoes into medium-sized pieces. Using a frying pan, fry the chopped onions and ginger (if using) in the butter-fat in the usual way. Add turmeric, salt and chilli powder (if using); after two or three minutes, add the cut potatoes and tomatoes, let these sizzle for ten minutes before adding the pea pods.

Add garam-masala, and after making sure that the curry is well cooked and dry, remove from the heat.

Although the preparation of the pea pods takes a little time, it is worthwhile, because the curry is quite tasty.

Mushroom Curry

450g (1lb) fresh white mushrooms
6 small potatoes
1 tablespoon set butter-fat
2 medium-sized onions, peeled
Small piece of ginger and a little
    chilli powder (optional)
2 dessertspoons broken coriander
    or any other fresh herbs

1 teaspoon turmeric
2½ teaspoons salt
3 medium-sized tomatoes
1 teaspoon garam-masala
1 tablespoon lemon juice

For 4 or 5 people
Soak the mushrooms in cold water for 15 minutes, scrape them lightly and
if too big, cut into halves and quarters. Wash under running water and drain.
Scrape the potatoes, keeping them whole. Heat the butter-fat in a saucepan,
add the thinly sliced onions, ginger (if using) and herbs, and fry gently for
five minutes: then add turmeric, salt and chilli powder (if using). Allow to
sizzle for a minute or two, then add the mushrooms, potatoes and sliced
tomatoes. Mix well, and if the juice is not required, let the mushrooms cook
uncovered, over medium heat for 30 minutes. Add garam-masala and
lemon juice; simmer for another 10 minutes, and then serve piping hot.

Curried mushrooms are very tasty, retain their flavour, and go very well
with a dish of curried lentils or beans.

INDIAN cooking

Peas and Mushroom Curry

The cooking method for this curry is exactly the same as for the previous recipe, the only difference being that a teacup of shelled peas is used instead of the potatoes.

French or Runner Bean Curry

1 tablespoon set butter-fat
1 medium-sized onion, peeled
A little ginger and ½ teaspoon
    chilli powder (optional)
1 teaspoon turmeric
2 teaspoons salt

2 tomatoes
450g (1lb) fresh young beans
2 medium-sized potatoes
1 teaspoon garam-masala
1 dessertspoon lemon juice

For 4 people
Place the butter-fat in a deep frying pan, and in this gently fry the thinly sliced onion and ginger (if using) for a few minutes. Add turmeric, salt and chilli powder (if using); let these sizzle for a couple of minutes, then add the sliced tomatoes. Mix well and fry until most of the liquid has gone. Remove the hard ends of the beans, wash them and cut them into 2.5cm (1in) long pieces. Wash and scrape the potatoes and cut into suitable sized pieces, and add both vegetables to the mixture in the frying pan. Mix well and cook with a loose lid on, until the beans and potatoes are tender – not broken. Then the lid should be taken off, and the curry should be cooked until the excess liquid has gone. Add garam-masala and lemon juice a few minutes before removing from the heat.

Young broad beans (pod and all) can be prepared by the same method.

Vegetable Dishes

Curried Cauliflower (Dry)

900g (2lb) cauliflower
4 small potatoes
7g (¼oz) ginger, fresh or dried
1 small onion, peeled
1½ tablespoons set butter-fat

1½ teaspoons turmeric
2 teaspoons salt
½ teaspoon chilli powder (optional)
1 teaspoon garam-masala

For 5 people
Slice the cauliflower into 5cm (2in) long thin pieces, taking care to keep some of the long stalk with the flower; wash and drain. Scrape and wash the potatoes, and if too large, cut them into medium-sized pieces. In a deep frying pan, fry the sliced ginger and onion in the butter-fat. Add turmeric and then put the slices of cauliflower and the pieces of potato in the pan, and allow to sizzle for 5–10 minutes, then add salt and chilli powder (if using). Keep covered over a low heat until tender, stirring frequently with a slice – not a spoon – to avoid crushing. Remove the lid and reduce the excess liquid. Add garam-masala five minutes before taking off the heat.

   This curry is a great favourite with most people, and will go well with any other curried dish, meat or otherwise.

Sweet Peppers

Stuffed Capsicums

1 teacup dal urad or red lentils
1 teacup water
2½ teaspoons salt
½ teaspoon turmeric
7g (¼oz) root ginger (fresh or
    dried) or a medium-sized
    onion, peeled

1½ tablespoons set butter-fat
1 level teaspoon garam-masala
1 tablespoon ground mango, or
    lemon juice
6 medium-sized peppers

To make the Stuffing

For 6 people

Pick and wash the dal urad or red lentils, and put them over a low heat with a teacup of water. Add 1½ teaspoons salt and the turmeric; cover the saucepan with a tight lid, and cook very gently until the lentils are soft and dry, then remove from the heat.

Fry the finely chopped ginger or onion in ½ tablespoon of butter-fat; add the cooked lentils, garam-masala and the ground mango or lemon juice; mix well, and let it cool down.

Wash and dry the peppers and, after making a slit in the middle of each one, stuff them with the lentil mixture. Heat the rest of the butter-fat in a large frying pan, and add the stuffed peppers. Sprinkle the rest of the salt on them and let them sizzle over medium heat for 15 minutes, turning them occasionally. Cover them up for a little while; after that, fry them until they are soft and partially brown.

The peppers can also be stuffed with potato mixture or minced meat.

How to make Potato Mixture

Boil four medium-sized potatoes in their jackets; when cool, peel and mash them well, and put them in the sizzling onion mixture. Add the same amount

of salt, turmeric, garam-masala and the ground mango or lemon juice as in the lentil mixture.

How to make the Minced Meat Stuffing

Cook 225g (½lb) of minced meat in a saucepan with a tight lid, using as little water as possible. Add salt and turmeric while it is cooking. The meat is ready to put into the sizzling onion mixture when it is tender and dry. Add garam-masala and ground mango or lemon juice.

    Two tomatoes and a tablespoon of breadcrumbs can also be mixed into this stuffing.

INDIAN cooking

Mixed Greens Purée

Sag

450g (1lb) ready-to-use spinach
450g (1lb) any other fresh greens
1 large turnip (not woody inside)
1 teacup water
2 teaspoons salt

½ teaspoon chilli powder
1 tablespoon set butter-fat
15g (½oz) fresh ginger or a
    medium-sized onion, peeled

For 6 people

Wash and cut as finely as you can the spinach, greens and the turnip. Heat half a teacup of water in a large heavy saucepan, and add the mixed greens. Add the salt and chilli powder, and cook (uncovered) for an hour over medium heat. When the excess water is reduced, mash the mixture well and remove from heat.

Using a large frying pan, fry the minced or finely chopped ginger or onion for a few minutes in the butter-fat, then add in the mashed greens. Mix well and keep stirring and mashing until the greens are smooth and dry.

Greens cooked in this way can be warmed up without losing flavour. Instead of mixing the greens, spinach or spring greens alone can be prepared by this method. Sag is a traditional Indian dish, and is particularly tasty when eaten with makki ki roti (see page 102) – bread made with maize flour, and dahi – milk-curd.

Spinach and Dal Urad or Yellow Split Peas

700g (1½lb) picked spinach
½ teacup of dal urad or split
   peas
1 teacup water
1 teaspoon turmeric
2 teaspoons salt

½ teaspoon chilli powder (optional
2 medium-sized onions, peeled or
   7g (¼oz) fresh ginger
1 tablespoon set butter-fat
1 teaspoon garam-masala

For 4 people
Wash the spinach under running water, and cut it as finely as you can. Sort and wash the dal or split peas and allow to soak for a few minutes. Boil the water in a saucepan, add the well-drained dal, turmeric and salt, and the chilli powder (if using). Cook for five minutes and then add the spinach. Keep over medium heat, stirring frequently, for about half an hour, until the excess moisture has gone, then remove from the heat. Place the chopped onions or ginger and butter-fat in a frying pan and fry gently until golden brown; add the garam-masala and the previously cooked spinach, mix well and keep over moderate heat for a few minutes before serving.

   This will go well with any other curried dish.

INDIAN cooking

Turnip Purée

Sag Shalgam

900g (2lb) turnips
½–1 teacup water
1 small piece of ginger (fresh) or
   root or a medium-sized onion,
   peeled

1 tablespoon set butter-fat
1½ teaspoons salt
½ teaspoon garam-masala
½ teaspoon chilli powder (optional)
1 teaspoon sugar (optional)

For 4 or 5 people

Peel the turnips (they should not be 'woody' inside), and cut them into small pieces. Heat half a teacup of water in a large saucepan, and add the turnips, cooking slowly for 30 minutes. When the turnips are quite soft, mash them well, remove from the heat and keep them by you. Fry the finely sliced ginger or onion in a frying pan, add the mashed turnip and the salt, garam-masala, chilli powder and sugar (if using). Fry until all the excess juice has dried out. In cold weather, this dish, like so many Indian dishes, does not lose its flavour if it is kept for a few hours and then warmed up.

Parsnips and swedes are also very tasty when cooked by this method. Swedes, however, need 45 minutes' cooking instead of 30 minutes before mashing.

We use turnips quite a lot in Punjab, and I have found that people, particularly the children, who dislike boiled turnips and swedes, take to this dish very well. Swedes are plentiful and cheap, and it is as well to make the most of them.

Turnip Curry

900g (2lb) white turnips
  (not woody)
1¼ tablespoons set butter-fat
1 medium-sized onion, peeled
7g (¼oz) ginger (fresh or dried)
2 tablespoons coriander or
  other fresh herbs

1 teaspoon turmeric
2 teaspoons salt
½ teaspoon chilli powder (optional)
2 tablespoons milk-curd or 1
  dessertspoon lemon juice
1 teaspoon garam-masala

For 4 people

Peel and cut the turnips into fairly small thin pieces; wash and drain. Place the butter-fat in a saucepan and fry therein the finely-sliced onion, ginger and broken-up coriander or herbs. Add turmeric, salt and chilli powder (if using); mix well and allow to sizzle for a few minutes. Then add the curd or lemon juice; let this simmer and dry up. Add the pieces of turnip; mix and cook for five minutes. Cover well, and cook over low heat for 30–40 minutes, stirring occasionally. If the curry begins to stick, sprinkle a little hot water over it. But sometimes turnips have too much juice in them, which can be dried off by turning the heat up higher and keeping the lid off for a few minutes. When the turnips are tender, break (don't mash) them with a spoon, and add garam-masala.

  Keep over the heat until the curry is perfectly dry, then serve hot with meat or vegetable dishes.

  Swedes are very tasty when prepared by the above method, but they take a little longer to cook.

INDIAN cooking

Curried Marrow

1 medium-sized tender marrow
2 onions
1 tablespoon set butter-fat
1 teaspoon turmeric
1½ teaspoons salt

1 teaspoon garam-masala
½ teaspoon chilli powder (optional)
2 large tomatoes
2 tablespoons curd or 1 tablespoon
   lemon juice

For 3 or 4 people
Scrape the marrow and cut into small pieces (not too small); unless the seeds
are very hard they can be left in. Wash well and let the pieces drain. Using
a saucepan, fry the onions, cut into large pieces, in the butter-fat over a low
heat and let them sizzle for a minute or two. Add the turmeric, salt, garam-
masala and chilli powder (if using). Mix well, add sliced tomatoes and fry
them for a few minutes; then add the curd or lemon juice. Mix and cook this
mixture until excess liquid is dried off and add the pieces of marrow. Mix in
well, and cook uncovered for 5 minutes. Then put the lid on, and cook for
another 15–20 minutes; uncover and let the excess liquid dry off.

    The marrow should be well cooked and dry before it is removed from the heat.

Curried Leeks

8 medium-sized leeks
4 varia (spicy dried lentil cakes
 – see page 95)
1 tablespoon set butter-fat
1 teaspoon turmeric
1 teaspoon salt
½ teaspoon garam-masala

½ teaspoon chilli powder (optional)
2 small pieces ginger
½ teacup hot water
3 medium-sized tomatoes
2 tablespoons milk-curd or
 1 dessertspoon lemon juice

For 4 people

Remove the rough heads and most of the green tails from the leeks, and make two or three cuts lengthwise in each one, taking care not to cut them through completely; wash them under running water and allow to drain.

Using a saucepan, fry the varhia (whole or broken in two or three pieces each) slowly in the butter-fat for 2–3 minutes. Add turmeric, salt, garam-masala, chilli powder (if using) and the chopped ginger. Mix well and let it sizzle for a minute or two. Then add the leeks, frying gently without a lid for a little while, and stirring occasionally, then pour in the hot water. Bring to the boil, turn the heat down quite low, cover and cook gently for the next 20 minutes. Next add the sliced tomatoes, milk-curd or lemon juice. Mix thoroughly, taking care not to crush the leeks. Simmer for 15–20 minutes.

INDIAN cooking

Stuffed Aubergines

2 medium-sized onions, peeled
1 small pepper
1 small piece of ginger and ½
   teaspoon chilli powder (optional)
1¼ tablespoons set butter-fat
1 teaspoon turmeric

2 teaspoons salt
1 teaspoon garam-masala
1 tablespoon ground mango or
   lemon juice
8 fairly small aubergines

For 4 people
Mince the onions, pepper and ginger (if using) together. Put a teaspoon of butter-fat in a small frying pan and slowly fry the onion mixture. Add the turmeric, 1½ teaspoons of salt, garam-masala, chilli powder and the ground mango or lemon juice. Fry this mixture well, so that no moisture is left in it, then remove from the heat.

    Wash and dry the aubergines, and make two deep cuts in each, keeping the tops and bottoms smooth. Stuff as much as possible of the fried onion mixture into these cuts, then loosely tie some clean cotton round each aubergine. Heat the rest of the butter-fat in a large, deep frying pan, and add the aubergines. Sprinkle the remaining ½ teaspoon of salt over them and fry gently, turning them with a slice every now and then. Cover them with an enamel plate for part of the time, so that they become tender. When well cooked (but not broken) and dry, remove from the heat and serve hot.

Aubergine Purée

Bhartha

2 large aubergines
1¼ tablespoons set butter-fat
2 medium-sized onions, peeled
1 piece of ginger and
   ½ teaspoon chilli powder
   (optional)

½ teaspoon turmeric
2 teaspoons salt
1 teaspoon garam-masala
225g (½lb) tomatoes
2 tablespoons freshly broken-up
   coriander or any other fresh herbs

For 4 people
Place the aubergines in a pan under a grill or at the top of the oven, turn frequently, holding them by their tops. The skin will gradually get black and the aubergines will become soft inside. They should be soft from top to bottom. Place under running water and carefully peel by hand. Drain the water out of them and mash well. Put the butter-fat into a frying-pan over a low heat; cut the onions and ginger (if using) into small pieces and fry them slowly until they are a light brown colour, then add turmeric, salt, garam-masala and chilli powder (if using). Mix well, then add the tomatoes cut into small pieces and the herbs. Let the mixture dry up while frying, and lastly add the aubergines. Fry the whole mixture for 5–10 minutes, stirring continuously. When the mixture is fairly solid, it is ready.

    Bhartha should be served hot, and will go with any juicy vegetable or meat dishes.

INDIAN cooking

Curried Cabbage

Band Gobhi

700g (1½lb) firm, whitish cabbage
A small piece of ginger, root or
    fresh, or 1 medium-sized onion,
    peeled
1 tablespoon set butter-fat

1 teaspoon turmeric
2 teaspoons salt
½ teaspoon chilli powder (optional)
1 teaspoon garam-masala

For 4 people
Shred the cabbage (not too small) and after washing well, allow to drain.
Using a large, heavy frying pan, fry the finely sliced ginger or onion in the
butter-fat. After a few minutes, add the turmeric, salt and chilli powder (if
using); mix well, and then put in the cabbage. To start with, fill the frying pan
to capacity, as during the cooking the cabbage will naturally shrink. Stir with
a slice (not a spoon) to prevent crushing. Cook without a lid over medium
heat for 15 minutes; then, when the excess liquid begins to dry off, cover the
frying pan with a lid or enamel plate. Continue to cook gently until cabbage
is tender, then uncover again. Fry quickly until the curry is quite dry, then add
garam-masala and mix well. When ready, the curried cabbage should be
perfectly dry, but not mashy.

   Brussels sprouts can be curried by the above method, but they should be
kept whole, not shredded.

Banana Curry

700g (1½lb) bananas (slightly
   under-ripe)
1 dessertspoon set butter-fat
½ teaspoon turmeric
½ teaspoon caraway seeds
   (optional)

1 teaspoon salt
½ teaspoon chilli powder (optional)
½ teaspoon garam-masala
2 tablespoons milk-curd or
   1 tablespoon milk and 1
   tablespoon lemon juice

For 3 people

After peeling the bananas, cut them into lengths about 2.5cm (1in) long.
Using a thick frying pan, heat the butter-fat, add the turmeric and caraway
seeds (if using). After a few minutes, add the pieces of banana, salt and chilli
powder (if using), mix and cook gently (uncovered) for 5–7 minutes. Add the
garam-masala and the milk-curd or milk and lemon juice. Stir with the end
of a spoon, taking care not to crush the bananas. Simmer for about another
7 minutes, until all the excess juice is dried up and the bananas are tender
but not broken: the curry will then be ready.

It should be served hot with curried meat or vegetable dishes.

INDIAN cooking

Beans, Pulses and Poppadoms

Split Black Beans

Dal Urad (Dry)

1½ teacups dal urad
  (see page 7)
1 tablespoon set butter-fat
2 medium-sized onions, peeled
A little chopped ginger and
  chilli powder (optional)
15g (½oz) broken-up fenugreek
  or any other fresh herbs

1 teaspoon turmeric
2½ teaspoons salt
225g (½lb) tomatoes
1¼ teacups hot water
1 teaspoon garam-masala

For 5 or 6 people

Sort and wash the dal and allow to soak for a little while. Using a thick saucepan, fry the thinly sliced onions, ginger (if using) and the herbs gently in the butter-fat for a few minutes. Care must be taken not to let these get really brown. Add turmeric, salt and chilli powder (if using); mix well and add sliced tomatoes. Let the mixture sizzle for a few minutes, and then add the washed and drained beans. Keep stirring for another five minutes, then pour in the hot water. Bring quickly to the boil, and after that you can either cook them (well covered) over a very low heat for 30–40 minutes, or better still, they can be placed (well covered) in a pre-heated oven (180°C/350°F/Gas 4) for the same length of time. The garam-masala can be mixed in with the beans a few minutes before removing from the heat.

  This dal is served hot, and the flavour is improved by squeezing a little lemon juice over it.

INDIAN cooking

Whole Black Beans

Whole Urad

1½ teacups urad (see page XX)
4½ teacups water
1½ teaspoons salt
1 teaspoon turmeric
7g (¼oz) fresh or dried ginger, or
   2 medium-sized onions, peeled

1 tablespoon set butter-fat
1½ teaspoons garam-masala
½ teaspoon chilli powder (optional)
2 tablespoons fresh chopped
   coriander or other fresh herbs

For 5 or 6 people
Sort and wash the whole urad, boil the water in a saucepan, and put them in. Add salt and turmeric, and cook over a low heat for an hour and a half.

Using a small frying pan, fry the ginger or onions in the butter-fat; add garam-masala, chilli powder (if using) and chopped coriander or other herbs. Allow to sizzle for a few minutes, and then add this to the urad in the saucepan. Mix well, and keep over a low heat for 10 minutes longer.

This dal is eaten with chapatis or rice, and is considered to be very nourishing.

Split Peas

Dal Channa

1 teacup dal channa (see page 7)
3 teacups water
1½ teaspoons salt
1 teaspoon turmeric
½ teaspoon chilli powder and a
  piece of ginger (optional)

1 tablespoon set butter-fat
1 medium-sized onion, peeled
2 tablespoons broken-up fenugreek,
  or other fresh herbs
1 teaspoon garam-masala

For 4 people

Sort and wash the dal, and let it soak for 30 minutes or so. Boil the water in a saucepan, and after draining the dal, add it to the water, together with salt, turmeric and chilli powder (if using). Bring to the boil, then turn heat down quite low and, keeping the lid on, cook until the dal is tender, which will take about an hour. Mix well with a spoon, without allowing the dal to get 'mashy'.

Place the butter-fat in a frying pan, and fry the chopped onions and ginger; add herbs and garam-masala just before taking off the heat. Pour this mixture onto the dal, which should now be ready for serving.

Dal urad and the yellow split peas which are widely available can be prepared by using the same ingredients and method. Some people mix dal channa and urad together, which makes the dish even tastier.

INDIAN cooking

Split Green Beans or Red Lentils

Dal Moong

1 teacup dal moong (see page 7)
2½ teacups water
1 dessertspoon set butter-fat
1 medium-sized onion, peeled
1 teaspoon garam-masala

2 tablespoons broken coriander
   or any other fresh herbs
1½ teaspoons salt
1 teaspoon turmeric
½ teaspoon chilli powder (optional)

For 4 people
The cooking method for this dal is exactly the same as for dal channa (see above), but the cooking time is reduced to just over 15 minutes, instead of 1 hour. This dal should also be served well garnished with fried onions, herbs and garam-masala.

This dish is considered to be very easily digested, and is often given (without the onion mixture and the chilli powder) to very young children, invalids and convalescents.

Red lentils can be prepared by the above method and with the same ingredients.

Whole Bengal Dried Peas

Kabli Channas

240g (8½oz) channas
  (see page 7)
2 medium-sized onions, peeled
4 small cloves of garlic, peeled
7g (¼oz) chopped ginger
2 fresh green chillies, or ½
  teaspoon chilli powder (optional)
2 tablespoons broken-up coriander
  or any other fresh herbs

1 teaspoon turmeric
2 teaspoons salt
1½ teaspoons garam-masala
1½ tablespoons set butter-fat
225g (½lb) tomatoes
40g (1½oz) tamarinds
  (or 3 tablespoons of lemon
  juice)

For 5 or 6 people
Sort, wash and soak the channas in ample water for at least 12 hours. Then you can either boil them in the same water over medium heat until they are very soft (almost splitting), or in a pressure cooker for 30 minutes, using a little less water than shown on the cooker chart.

Pour the stock from the channas into a jug. Mince the onions, garlic, ginger, chillies (if using) and herbs together; mix in the turmeric, salt, chilli powder and garam-masala. Heat the butter-fat in a saucepan and gently fry the mixture. Add thinly sliced tomatoes and allow to sizzle for 7 minutes. Add the channas, mix well and keep over medium heat for a little longer. Add ½ teacup of the stock and, when gently boiling, add tamarind juice, which is prepared as follows.

Rinse the tamarinds and pour on them 1½ teacups of stock from the jug (hot water instead of stock, if necessary). Soak the fruit well and remove all pulp; strain through a sieve (not too fine), and add to the channas. If tamarind is not available, lemon juice could be used. Let the curry simmer on the top of the cooker or in the oven for 20–30 minutes (pre-heated to 150°C/300°F/Gas 2). Channas are tastier if prepared a few hours in advance, then heated through and served piping hot. They are delicious with savoury rice and with various dry vegetable or meat dishes. Some people improve the flavour still more by cooking a few pieces of lamb or mutton with the channas.

Tamarind is available from larger supermarkets but channas have to be obtained from an Indian grocer. There is no real substitute for them.

INDIAN cooking

Haricot and Other Dried Beans

1 teacup dried beans
1½–2 teaspoons salt
5 teacups water
1 medium-sized onion, peeled
Some fresh herbs and 1
    medium-sized red pepper
7g (¼oz) ginger, fresh or root,
    and ½ teaspoon chilli powder
    – if desired

2 flakes of garlic
1 tablespoon set butter-fat
1 teaspoon turmeric
1 teaspoon garam-masala
2 medium-sized tomatoes
A few pieces of meat or marrow
    bones – if desired
50g (2oz) tamarinds, or 1 tablespoon
    lemon juice

For 4 to 5 people
Sort, wash and soak the beans for 8 hours; then rinse, and put them on to boil, with a teaspoon of salt and 4 teacups of water and the meat or bones, over a low heat, stirring occasionally. Boil until quite tender, which will take about 1¼ hours, then remove from the heat.

Using another saucepan, fry the chopped onions, herbs, ginger (if using) and garlic in the butter-fat; add tumeric, 1 teaspoon salt, garam-masala and the chilli powder (if using). Let this sizzle for a few minutes, then add the sliced tomatoes, let them mix and get tender. Next add the beans and meat without the stock, mix and fry gently for five minutes; then add the stock. Rinse and soak the tamarinds in a teacup of water (hot) for 2–3 minutes, then rub the fruit with your fingers so that all the pulp comes off the stones. Pour this pulp and the juice of the tamarinds onto the simmering beans. If tamarind is not available, then lemon juice can be used.

The cooking time will vary with different kinds of dried beans.

Curried beans are very tasty served with rice pulao or other vegetable dishes, and should be served hot.

Rissoles Made with Dal or Lentils

Mongorhis (Mumgauris) I

1 teacup dal moong, urad
   (see page 7), or red lentils
1 teaspoon salt
½ teaspoon turmeric

½ teaspoon garam-masala
1 teaspoon caraway seeds
½ teaspoon chilli powder (optional)
Some oil or fat for frying

For 18 or 20 mongorhis
Sort, wash and soak the dal for 18–24 hours. After that, drain it well and, placing a portion of it in a large mortar, crush it as much as possible with the pestle. When all the dal has been thus treated, put it in a mixing bowl, add the other ingredients except the oil or fat, and beat the mixture for several minutes. Heat the oil or fat to smoking point and, taking some of the mixture, either by hand or in a spoon, drop it into the smoking fat. Fry 5 or 6 mongorhis at a time over medium heat.

    These mongorhis can also be served hot or cold at tea time, or they can be curried by the same method and using the same ingredients as in the following recipe.

INDIAN cooking

Rissoles made with Dal or Lentils

Mongorhis (Mumgauris) II

1 teacup dal moong, urad	½ teaspoon garam-masala
(see page 7) or red lentils	½ teaspoon chilli powder (optional)
1½ teacups warm water	1 teaspoon caraway seeds
1½ teaspoons salt	Some oil or fat for frying

For 24 small mongorhis
Sort the dal and rub it with a clean cloth; grind in a coffee mill, and pass the flour through a sieve. The roughage can be used in soups and you should now have ¾ teacup of flour. Gradually add the warm water to make a thick batter. Beat with a spoon for several minutes, then add salt, garam-masala, chilli powder (if using) and the caraway seeds. Let stand for one hour, then beat thoroughly again. Heat the oil or fat in a deep frying pan or chip pan over a medium heat; when smoking hot, drop in small portions of the lentil mixture carefully with a spoon or your clean hands. Fry 4 or 5 mongorhis at a time over medium heat. When golden brown all round, remove from the pan, drain well and place on a large shallow dish. Mongorhis can be served as they are, hot or cold, at tea time, or they can be curried by the following method:

For the curry

1 medium-sized onion, peeled	1 teaspoon garam-masala
1 medium-sized red pepper, or	½ teaspoon chilli powder
1 tablespoon fresh chopped	4 large tomatoes
herbs	1 teacup hot water
1 tablespoon butter-fat	½ teacup milk-curd or 1 tablespoon
1 teaspoon turmeric	lemon juice
1 teaspoon salt	

Chop and fry the onion and red pepper or herbs in the butter-fat in a heavy saucepan; add turmeric, salt, garam-masala and chilli powder; mix well and then add the sliced tomatoes. Let the mixture sizzle for a few minutes and then add the mongorhis. Stir well, and leave over a low heat for a little while longer. Add hot water and the curd, bring to the boil, and after covering it, allow to simmer for 10–15 minutes.
   This curry is very tasty and goes down well with rice pulao.

Small Dried Spicy Lentil Cakes

Varia (Baria; the spelling Waria is also known)

1 teacup dal urad (see page 7)
   or ordinary red lentils
2 tablespoons dal urad or
   lentil flour
1 teaspoon caraway seeds
1½ teaspoons garam-masala
1 tablespoon coriander seeds

2 teaspoons salt
½ teaspoon turmeric
1 teaspoon chilli powder (optional)
A small lump (about the size of a
   haricot bean) of asafoetida
   (optional)

For 18 varia
Sort and wash the dal or lentils, and soak for 18–24 hours; then drain them and, putting a portion at a time into a large mortar, crush them with the pestle as much as you can. When completed, place them in a mixing bowl, add the flour (made by grinding the lentils in a coffee mill) and the rest of the ingredients. The asafœtida should be crushed before mixing. Beat and knead the mixture, then leave it in a warm place for 2–4 hours. Then knead it once again, and shape the varia by getting some of the mixture in your hand and letting it drop onto a well-greased plate. Continue the process until all the mixture is used up. Place the varia in the sun to dry, or if there is no possibility of drying them in the sun, they can be dried in an airing-cupboard. When perfectly dry, store them in a well-covered tin.

    Varias are very tasty when curried with a few pieces of potato. They are used in making varia pulao, and one or two varias can be added in the following curries: fresh French beans, runner beans, broad beans, peas, marrow and leeks, but care should be taken to fry the varias in the butter-fat with the onion mixture and cook in ½ teacup of water before adding the other vegetables.

INDIAN cooking

Small Dried Rice Puffs

Phul-varia

225g (½lb) fine ground rice
1.2 litres (2 pints) water
2 teaspoons salt
1 teaspoon baking powder

1–2 teaspoons caraway seeds
    (optional)
Butter-fat or oil for frying

For 36 phul-varia

Sieve the ground rice and keep it by you. Boil the water in a large, thick aluminium saucepan; turn the heat down low and mix in handfuls of ground rice, stirring all the time with a large spoon. Add salt, baking powder and the caraway seeds (if using). Mix well for a minute or two, breaking up any lumps there may be; cover with a tight lid and keep over the lowest possible heat for nearly an hour. Remove from the heat, spread a clean teacloth over a large tray and, when the mixture is cool enough to handle, take about a tablespoon of it and place it on the cloth, carefully keeping it in a round shape. Repeat the process until all the mixture is finished.

Leave these phul-varia to dry in the sun, or in an airing cupboard. If desired, the mixture can be shaped into long strips like cheese straws; but you will need to rub in a little edible oil to prevent the mixture from sticking to your hands.

When they are thoroughly dried, store the phul-varia in a tin. Phul-varia should be fried quickly in deep smoking fat or oil just before serving. They rise to double or treble their original size, and are crisp and very tasty to serve at tea time.

Poppadoms made with Dal Urad or Red Lentil Flour

Papars

225g (½lb) fine dal urad
    (see page 7) or red lentil flour
1 teaspoon salt
1 level dessertspoon baking powder
½ teacup warm water
2 tablespoons, or more, of edible
    edible oil or warm fat

1 teaspoon caraway seeds
1 teaspoon crushed cardomon
    seeds
1 teaspoon or more of crushed
    (not ground) black pepper
1 teaspoon chilli powder (optional)

For 15 papars
First set aside about a dessertspoon of the flour for use later on, then place
the remainder in a mixing bowl and add salt. Mix the baking powder in the
water (in India we use a kind of cooking soda) and gradually add this to the
flour, and mix into a stiff dough. Place the dough on a breadboard and
pound it vigorously with a pestle for 15 minutes, using generous dabs of
edible oil to prevent sticking. The expert papar makers bang the dough on
the board as if threshing corn. Mix in the spices and chilli powder (if using)
and pound once again. Indeed, the more you pound it, the lighter the
papars will be. Shape the whole of the dough into a long sausage, then cut
into small portions. Place these and the remainder of the flour in a bowl, and
cover them well with the flour.

INDIAN cooking

How to shape the papars

Take a portion of the flour-covered dough, grease it slightly and shape it round. Then roll it out so that it is as thin and round as possible (very thin indeed), using more oil if necessary. Roll out the rest of the portions similarly, place them all separately on a large cooling rack, and dry them in the sun or in a hot airing cupboard. They will only take a few hours to dry and should not be kept in the cupboard too long. Papars will always have a shiny, greasy surface and should be stored in a covered tin. They can be baked slowly on both sides on a gas ring (of course, a charcoal fire is best), or they can be fried in smoking oil or fat. Crisp and crunchy, they are served with drinks, with main meals, or at tea time. They can be made quite plain, i.e., you can leave out the spices if these are not wanted.

Papar making is an art in itself, and needs a lot of practice to get perfect results, but it is certainly worth trying.

Poppadoms made with Sago

Papar Sagudana

225g (½lb) sago
900ml (1½ pints) water
1½ teaspoons salt

½ teaspoon ground pepper
(black or white)

For 32 poppadoms
Wash the sago in cold water once or twice, then drain it well. Bring the water to the boil in a large, heavy aluminium saucepan and stir in the well-washed sago. Add salt and pepper, and cook slowly for 15 minutes, stirring all the time. The sago should by now be cooked and swollen, and can be removed from the heat.

Arrange a clean cloth on a large tray and spread a heaped tablespoon of the mixture in a thin round shape on the cloth. Repeat the process until all the mixture is used. Dry in the same way as described in the previous recipe; but poppadoms take much longer to dry and should be carefully removed from the cloth before they become really dry. If they do get stuck, dampen the cloth from the back, and gently persuade them away from it.

Poppadoms must be thoroughly dry before storing. Apart from this, they are very easy to make and are fried in deep smoking fat just before serving.

They are very light and crisp, and attractive looking; and are great favourites with children.

INDIAN cooking

Breads

Breads

Unleavened Indian Wholemeal Bread

Chapatis

2½ teacups wholemeal flour
1 teaspoon salt

About 1 teacup water
1 tablespoon set butter-fat (optional)

For 10–12 chapatis

Sieve 2 teacups of the flour into a mixing bowl (saving ½ teacup of flour for shaping the chapatis); add salt and mix into a loose dough by gradually adding the water. Pound and knead with your hands for several minutes, for the more the bread is kneaded, the lighter it will be. Leave the dough for at least 1 hour, then knead once again and, if necessary, sprinkle a little more water on it. Shape the chapatis by breaking off a small portion of the dough, shaping it into a ball and, with the help of a little dry flour, roll it out thin and round like a pancake. Heat the 'tava' (an iron hot-plate, or use a griddle) and grease it slightly. Flatten the chapati by tossing it from one hand to the other, then place it on the hot-plate or griddle and bake over medium heat, first on one side (only slightly this time), and then the other. Turn again, and encourage it to rise by pressing the sides of the chapati with a clean cloth; the chapati usually comes right up like a balloon. It should be baked all round before it is removed from the hot-plate or griddle; the baking can be finished off under the hot grill after it has been partially baked on the hot-plate or griddle. All this has to be done fairly quickly, as too slow cooking will make the chapatis go hard. If butter-fat is used, it should be warmed up and then spread sparingly with a spoon on one side of each chapati.

Chapatis are good to eat (with or without butter) just as they are removed from the heat, still puffed up. For keeping them hot, it is best to pile one on top of the other, and wrap a cloth round them. Then this bundle can be placed in a deep ovenproof dish, covered, and kept in a very low oven (about 150°C/300°F/Gas 2).

Chapatis are the mainstay of the majority of Indian folk, particularly Punjabis, and it is surprising how much nourishment is derived from them. In addition, I must point out that dogs are very fond of them and thrive on them wonderfully well.

Note: The hot-plate or a griddle must be used for baking chapatis; a grill is not suitable.

101

INDIAN cooking

Bread made with Maize Flour

Makki Ki Roti

4 teacups maize flour
1½ teaspoons salt

1–1½ teacups water
1 dessertspoon (or more) butter-fat

For 5 or 6 rotis
Sieve the flour, which is of yellowish colour and rather coarse. The roughage should be kept for another use. Add salt, and separating enough flour for one roti, make it into a stiff dough by gradually adding a little of the water. Mix and knead for a little while, then shape the roti, thick and round, on your hand, and place it on the well-greased 'tava' (hot iron plate) or griddle. Continue the flattening by pressing it all round with the palm of your hand, taking care not to break it. Cook fairly slowly on both sides; the edges of this roti are usually uneven. Warmed butter-fat can be thinly spread on it when the roti is removed from the heat. The dough for each of the rotis is prepared separately as you go along.

Some people prefer to mix a little warm butter-fat and chopped fenugreek into the dough, the inclusion of which makes the roti even tastier.

Makki ki roti is served hot or warm, usually with sag (mixed greens) and dahi (milk-curd), and is considered to be very nourishing.

Pure maize or millet flour is available from larger supermarkets and health food stores, as well as corn merchants. Polenta, the maize flour, which can be purchased from Italian delicatessens, as well as supermarkets, is quite suitable for making makki ki roti providing it is fine enough.

Bread made with Millet Flour

Bajre Ki Roti

This is prepared in the same way as makki ki roti, except that millet flour is used instead of maize. Bajre ki roti can be made crisp and sweet by adding some warm butter-fat (1 tablespoon) and 100g (¼lb) demerara sugar, which is dissolved in the water before mixing it with the dough.

Leavened Bread

Khamiri Moti Roti

For Khamir (home-made yeast)

100g (4oz) plain flour (not
    wholemeal)
2 teaspoons sugar
1 dozen black peppercorns (whole)

2 tablespoons slightly warm
    milk-curd
2 tablespoons warm water

Sift the flour into a basin. Add sugar, peppercorns and the milk-curd.
Mix well with the warm water, beat for a few minutes and leave in a warm
place for 18 hours.

For Bread

4 teacups flour (wholemeal or
    plain)
The khamir (home-made yeast),
    available from Indian stores

2 teaspoons salt
1 teaspoon sugar (optional)
About 1½ teacups warm water

For 6 rotis
Sift the flour in a mixing bowl; add yeast (the peppercorns can be taken out
and used again), salt and sugar (if using). Rub the mixture with your hands
and gradually add some of the warm water to form a dough. Knead for
several minutes. Cover with a cloth and leave in a warm place to rise. When
the dough is nearly double its original size, it is ready. Using a little warm
water, knead the dough again for a minute or two, then, with the help of a
little dry flour, shape each roti on the palm of your hand, keeping it fairly
thick and round. Place it on the already heated iron plate (or griddle), and
cook over medium heat, turning it once or twice. When nearly done, place
on a grill pan under a pre-heated grill and toast well on both sides. This
bread can be fried in deep hot fat instead of baking. Also, after the dough
has risen, some warm butter fat or other seasoning can be added to it.
Kamiri roti is easily digested and is very tasty.

INDIAN cooking

Puffed Bread

Parathas

2½ teacups wholemeal flour
About 1 teacup water

2 tablespoons or more set butter-fat
½ teaspoon salt

For 10 parathas
Use 2 teacups of the flour (saving ½ teacup for shaping the parathas) and prepare the dough for the parathas as for chapatis (see page 101), and let the dough stand. Heat the butter-fat and have it by you. Break off a piece of the dough, shape it into a ball and, with the help of a little dry flour, roll it out (not too thinly). Using a spoon, spread some warm butter-fat on it, then fold it over and spread a little more butter-fat on the fresh layer. Do this two or three times and eventually roll the paratha out fairly thinly so that it is either round or V-shaped. Grease the hot iron plate or griddle well, and put the paratha on it; when one side is partially cooked, turn it and spread butter-fat liberally on it; do the same to the other side. When ready, the parathas should be a golden-brown colour and well soaked in butter-fat.

They should be served piping hot with vegetable or meat dishes.

Parathas stuffed with Potato Mixture

For the Stuffing

2 large potatoes
1 dessertspoon butter-fat, plus
    extra for spreading
1 small onion, peeled
2 tablespoons coriander or
    other fresh herbs
A small piece of ginger and ½
    teaspoon chilli powder (optional)

1½ teaspoons salt
1 teaspoon garam-masala
1 tablespoon ground mango or
    1 dessertspoon lemon juice
Dry flour for rolling out

For 10 parathas
Boil the potatoes in their jackets; when cool, peel and mash them. Heat the butter-fat in a frying pan and fry the minced or finely chopped onion, herbs and ginger (if using) slowly for a few minutes. Add salt, garam-masala, chilli powder (if using) and ground mango or lemon juice. Mix in the already prepared potatoes, and let sizzle for two or three minutes. Remove from the heat and allow to cool.

The ingredients and the preparation of the dough are the same as for plain parathas.

After rolling the paratha out – not too thinly – spread the warm butter-fat on it as before and place a tablespoon or more of the prepared potato mixture in the centre. Fold all round and then, with the help of some dry flour, roll the paratha out as thinly and round as you can. Cook the stuffed parathas in the same way as the plain ones.

These parathas are very tasty eaten with dahi (milk-curd).

INDIAN cooking

Paratha stuffed with Peas

For the Stuffing

1 dessertspoon butter-fat
1 medium-sized onion, peeled
A little ginger and ½ teaspoon
    chilli powder
1–2 tablespoons broken-up
    coriander or other fresh herbs

1 medium-sized tomato
1–1½ teaspoons salt
1 teaspoon garam-masala
1½–2 teacups freshly shelled peas
1 dessertspoon ground mango or
    lemon juice (optional)

For 10 parathas
Put the butter-fat in a saucepan and fry the minced or finely chopped onion,
ginger and the herbs in it gently. Add sliced tomatoes, salt, garam-masala
and chilli powder; mix well and then add the washed and well-drained peas.
Let these sizzle for a few minutes, cover and cook over a low heat until the
peas are tender. The excess liquid can be reduced by turning the heat up
higher. Mash the peas slightly, add the ground mango or lemon juice and
use when cool.

Parathas Stuffed with Cauliflower

For the Stuffing

1½–2 teacups finely grated
   cauliflower
1 teaspoon garam-masala
1–1½ teaspoons salt

7g (¼oz) grated ginger (fresh
   or dried) and ½ teaspoon
   chilli powder (optional)

For 10 parathas
Finely grate only the flower part and the very tender stalks of the cauliflower
(the rest can be kept for another use). Place the grated cauliflower on a large
plate, mix in the rest of the ingredients and stuff the parathas with this
mixture immediately. This stuffing cannot be prepared in advance.

INDIAN cooking

Parathas stuffed with Indian, Chinese or Ordinary Radishes

For the Stuffing

1–1½ teacups grated radishes
7g (¼oz) root ginger (fresh or dried)
½ teaspoon chilli powder
1½–2 teaspoons salt

1–2 teaspoons garam-masala
1 tablespoon dried and crushed
    pomegranate seeds (from
    Indian stores)

For 10 parathas
Thoroughly wash, drain and grate the radishes, and squeeze excess juice out of them. Add grated ginger and the rest of the ingredients. Stuff the parathas with this mixture immediately because this stuffing becomes too watery if prepared in advance.

The large red or white Chinese radishes, when in season, are best for this dish. Ordinary large radishes can be used, if desired.

Indian radishes are generally white and are sometimes even larger than carrots. They can be obtained from Indian stores and some supermarkets.

These parathas are usually eaten with thick dahi (milk-curd).

Indian Fried Bread

Puris

3 teacups wholemeal flour
1 dessertspoon butter-fat
1 teaspoon salt
About 1¼ teacups warm water

Dry flour
225g (½lb) fat, or its equivalent in
   oil, for frying

For 14–18 puris.
Sieve the flour in a large mixing bowl, heat the butter-fat and add this to the bowl with the salt; rub in with your hands and then make it into a stiff dough by gradually adding the warm water. Knead for a few minutes.

To shape the Puris
Take a little of the dough, make into a ball and then, with the help of a little dry flour, roll it out round and fairly thin. Repeat the process until all the puris are rolled out; keep them separate from each other. Using a deep karhai or chip pan, heat the fat or oil to nearly smoking point and fry each puri separately fairly quickly over medium heat. Encourage it to rise by slightly pressing the sides with the slice or turner after the puri is partially cooked and by splashing some of the hot fat in the pan on top of it. When the puri has risen (some only rise slightly) and is golden brown on both sides, it is ready. Drain well and place in a warm, shallow dish. After they have been fried, the puris can be kept warm in a very low pre-heated oven (about 150°C/300°F/Gas 2). They are usually eaten hot, though in summer some people like them cold or merely warm. They are eaten with most of the Indian dishes, particularly with semolina halva, kabli channas and dry potato curry.

INDIAN cooking

Indian Fried Bread, Leavened

Khamiri Puri

100g (4oz) plain flour (not
   wholemeal)
1 tablespoon home-made khamir
   yeast (see page 103)
½ teaspoon salt

1½ teaspoons sugar
1 teaspoon set butter-fat
½ teacup warm milk
Some oil or fat for frying

For 6 Puris
Sieve the flour in a mixing bowl; add yeast, salt, sugar and the warmed-up
butter-fat. Mix into a dough by gradually adding the warm milk. Knead for
several minutes, and leave in a warm place for 2–3 hours. Then, with the
help of a little warm water, knead the dough again. Divide into 6 and roll
each section into small round puris (not too thinly), and fry them in deep fat
over medium heat.

   These puris are light and very delicious.

Another Variety of Fried Bread

Khasta Puri

1½ teacups wholemeal flour
1 teacup self-raising flour
1 teaspoon set butter-fat

1 teaspoon salt
Just over ½ teacup warm water
Some oil or fat for frying

For 10 puris
Sieve the flour and mix in the butter-fat and salt. Gradually add the warm water and mix into a stiff dough, knead for several minutes and then leave covered for 15 minutes. Break off a small portion of the dough and, after shaping it into a ball, roll it out fairly thinly and round. Repeat until the dough is finished. Heat the oil or fat in a chip pan and, when smoking hot, fry each puri separately in it, fairly quickly, turning frequently so that the puris are well fried on both sides. When they are of an almond brown colour, drain them well and place in a shallow dish. Serve them hot.

Puris usually rise up like a balloon and are very tasty when eaten with various Indian dishes.

INDIAN cooking

Puri with Potato Pastry

2 medium-sized potatoes (about
    225g/8oz after peeling and
    cooking)
225g (8oz) plain flour (not
    wholemeal)

2 teaspoons salt
½ teacup warm water
Some oil or fat for frying

For 14–15 puris
Boil the potatoes in their jackets and remove from the heat when just tender.
Allow to cool and, after skinning them, mash thoroughly. Knead them for a
few minutes, sieve in the flour, add salt and rub the mixture with your hands,
making it into a stiff pastry by gradually adding the warm water. Knead and
roll again as for ordinary puris. Heat the fat or oil in a chip pan and fry each
puri separately over *medium* heat, encouraging them to rise by spooning the
hot fat over them. When golden brown on both sides, drain the puris and
place in a shallow dish.

    The puris can be served hot or cold, and are very delicious when eaten
with kabli channas or curried haricot or other dried beans.

Another Variety of Fried Bread

Luchchi

*100g (4oz) plain flour (not
    wholemeal)*
15g (½oz) butter-fat
1 teaspoon salt

Nearly ½ teacup warm water
Flour for rolling out
Some oil or fat for frying

For 6 or 7 luchchis
Sieve the flour into a mixing bowl and rub in the fat. Add salt and make into a very stiff pastry by adding the warm water. Pound and knead for several minutes. Divide the pastry into 6 or 7 portions, shape these into balls and roll each one out – with the help of a little dry flour – very thinly and round. Get them all ready and then fry them separately and fairly quickly in deep hot fat. Drain them thoroughly and serve warm or cold.

INDIAN cooking

Stuffed Puris

Kachauris

The pastry for kachauris is prepared in the same way and with the same ingredients as for plain puris (page 109). They are rolled out slightly thicker and smaller and, after stuffing with the following mixtures, are fried as ordinary puris.

They can be stuffed with the potato, lentil or pea mixtures, as given in the recipe for stuffed parathas (pages 105–08).

INDIAN cooking

Milk-curd Recipes

Savoury Lentil Rissoles in Curd

Dahi Barhe

1 teacup dal urad, moong
  (page 7) or red lentils
1½–2 teaspoons salt
1 teaspoon caraway seeds
Some oil or fat for frying

1.2 litres (2 pints) fresh thick
  milk-curd
1 teaspoon garam-masala
1 teaspoon chilli powder
1 dessertspoon chopped mint or
  onions

For 4–5 people

Wash and soak the pulses in plenty of water overnight. Drain well the next day, and crush and pound them in a pestle and mortar a little at a time, as when making monghoris (page 93–4). Mix 1 teaspoon of salt and ½ teaspoon caraway seeds with the crushed pulses. Using a chip pan, bring the oil or fat to nearly smoking point; take a little of the mixture, flatten it slightly and over medium heat fry 3 or 4 rissoles at a time, until they are of a light brown colour on both sides. When all are done, rinse them in cold water to soften and get thoroughly cold.

Whisk the milk-curd, place it in a glass or china dish, add the remainder of the salt, garam-masala, caraway seeds, chilli powder and the chopped mint (or onions). Squeeze and flatten the rissoles and place them in the curd mixture. They should be ready to serve after 15 minutes. To improve the appearance of this dish, some people sprinkle a little ground paprika (which is not 'hot' at all) on the top.

This dish is served cold and tamarind chutney is often served with it.

INDIAN cooking

A Curd Preparation Similar to Soup

Dahi Carhi I

For Pakoris

2–3 tablespoons besan or split-pea
   flour
½ teaspoon salt

½ teaspoon garam-masala
2–3 tablespoons warm water
Some oil or fat for frying

For Curry

1 tablespoon set butter-fat
A dozen small spring onions
2 tablespoons broken-up coriander
   or other herbs
1–2 fresh green chillis or ½
   teaspoon chilli powder (if desired)
1 teaspoon turmeric
1–1½ teaspoons salt

2 tablespoons besan (split-pea flour)
1 teacup water
1 teacup milk
2 teacups curd which has been kept
   for a day or two, or lassi (whey)
1 tablespoon lemon juice (optional)
1 teaspoon garam-masala
1 teaspoon caraway seeds

For 4–5 people
To make pakoris

Sieve 2–3 tablespoons of besan or split-pea flour into a small mixing bowl;
add salt and garam-masala, and make the mixture into a thick batter by
gradually adding the warm water. Beat hard and allow to stand for a few
minutes. Heat the oil or fat in a chip pan to nearly boiling point. Beat the batter
once again and, taking some of it in your hand, drop small portions into the
hot fat. Fry as many pakoris as you can at a time over medium heat: keep them
on the move and, when they are a golden brown colour, remove them from
the pan and drain. Repeat the process until all the mixture is used up.

Milk-curd Recipes

To make the curry

Using a saucepan, fry gently in the butter-fat the onions, herbs and the green chillis (if using). Add turmeric and salt, and after a few minutes add the already prepared pakoris. Let these sizzle for 2 or 3 minutes.

Sieve the two tablespoons of besan into a small bowl, add a little of the water and make it into a batter. Gradually add the rest of the water and the milk and well-beaten curd or lassi (whey). If the curd is not tart enough, 1 tablespoon of lemon juice should be added to the mixture. Pour this liquid onto the sizzling pakoris, bring to the boil and then turn the heat up to medium. Keep stirring until the curry thickens, then continue cooking gently for 20 or 30 minutes. Add garam-masala and caraway seeds before removing from the heat.

The flavour of dahi carhi is improved by keeping it in a pre-heated low oven (150°C/300°F/Gas 2) for a little while after it has been cooked. It is usually served hot, and goes well with rice pulao.

INDIAN cooking

A Curd Preparation Similar to Soup

Dahi Carhi II

2 tablespoons besan (split-pea flour)
   or 1½ tablespoons cornflour
1 teacup water
1 teacup milk
2 teacups curd which has been
   kept for a day or two
1 tablespoon set butter-fat
6 small onions, peeled and
   chopped
2 medium-sized red peppers
   (optional)

5 small potatoes
1 teaspoon turmeric
1½ teaspoons salt
2 tablespoons broken-up coriander
   or other herbs
1 teaspoon caraway seeds
   (optional)
1 teaspoon chilli powder (optional)
1 teaspoon garam-masala
1 tablespoon lemon juice (optional)

For 4 or 5 people

Sieve the split-pea flour or cornflour into a mixing bowl, and make into a thin paste with some of the water. Mix in the milk, the milk-curd and the rest of the water. Keep this in a jug. Using a saucepan, fry in the butter-fat the onions, thick pieces of red pepper (if using) and the well-scraped potatoes for a few minutes. Add turmeric, salt, herbs, caraway seeds and the chilli powder (if using); cover the saucepan and cook gently until the vegetables are tender. Then add the curd mixture from the jug, bring to the boil and keep stirring until the curry thickens. After that, it can either be cooked, well covered, over a low heat for 30–40 minutes or, better still, it can be placed with the lid on in the oven (190°C/375°F/Gas 5) for the same length of time. Mix in the garam-masala about ten minutes before removing from the heat.

   If the curd is not tart enough, a tablespoon of lemon juice can be added to the curd mixture. Also, for a change, a few pieces of cauliflower, or varhia (dried lentil cakes, see page 95) can be used instead of potatoes, but whatever you put in, it must be allowed to tenderize before adding the curd mixture.

   This dish should be served piping hot, and goes very well with savoury rice pulao.

Potatoes in Curd

Raita Alu

2 large potatoes
1.2 litres (2 pints) fresh thick
    milk-curd
1½ teaspoons caraway seeds

1 teaspoon garam-masala
1 teaspoon chilli powder (optional)
1½ teaspoons salt

For 8 people
Boil the potatoes in their jackets. When cool, skin them and cut into fairly small pieces. Beat the milk-curd and mix in the rest of the ingredients. Add the potatoes and mix well with a spoon.

Raita is always served cold – indeed if it could be placed in a refrigerator for a short time before using the flavour would be improved.

Raita Mint and Onion

Made as raita alu, with the addition of 3 medium-sized onions, finely sliced, and 3 tablespoons of coarsely chopped mint.

Raita Cucumber

Made as raita alu, with the addition of 1 medium-sized cucumber, raw and grated.

Raita Marrow

Ingredients as for raita alu, with the addition of 1 small marrow. The marrow should be peeled, grated, slightly boiled, cooled down and squeezed before it is added to the curd mixture. Any large seeds should be removed, if they are too hard.

INDIAN cooking

Raita Aubergine

Ingredients as for raita alu, with the addition of three medium-sized aubergines.

Place the aubergines under a grill or on top of the cooker; turn frequently and, when their skins turn black and they are soft inside, place under running water and carefully peel by hand. When cool, mash well and add to the curd mixture.

Savoury Drops in Curd

Raita Pakori

For Pakoris

4 tablespoons besan (split-pea
   flour)
1 teaspoon salt

¾ teacup water
Some frying oil

Other ingredients as for raita alu

For 8 people
Make a thick batter of the ingredients, beat well and allow to stand for 10 minutes. Bring the oil to boiling point in a deep frying pan. Place some batter on a slice with large round holes and shake through the holes into the pan. Keep the pakoris on the move whilst frying and, when they are of a golden-brown colour, remove and allow to drain while a new batch is cooking. When cold, soften with tepid water and add to the curd mixture.

Milk-curd Recipes

Sweet Raitas

Raita Banana

1.2 litres (2 pints) fresh milk-curd
5–6 ripe yellow bananas

3–4 tablespoons sugar (preferably caster)

For 8 people
Beat the curd and place it in a glass dish. Peel and cut the bananas into thin, round pieces and place them in the curd. Stir in the sugar and serve either as an after-dinner sweet or as ordinary raita.

Raita Sultanas

4–6 tablespoons sultanas
1.2 litres (2 pints) fresh milk-curd

3–4 tablespoons sugar (preferably caster)

For 8 people
Wash and soak the sultanas for nearly 30 minutes before putting them in the well-beaten milk-curd. Add sugar and serve in the same way as banana raita.

INDIAN cooking

Sweetmeats

Laddoo Boondi

For mixture, etc.

1½ teacups besan or fine split-pea
    flour (weighed after sieving)
½ teaspoon saffron (for colour
    and fragrance)
Just over ½ teacup milk and
    water mixed together
250g (9oz) butter-fat, or any other
    clarified fat

1 dessertspoon finely sliced pistachio
    kernels or almond nuts
1 dessertspoon desiccated coconut
½ teaspoon cardamom seeds (not
    crushed) or grated nutmeg
Three slices or turners with medium-
sized holes will be needed

For syrup

Just over 1½ teacups sugar

1½ teacups water

For 20 medium-sized laddoos.
Place the sieved flour in a small mixing bowl. Soak the saffron in a dessertspoon of water, and mix half of this in with the flour. Gradually add the warm milk and water, mixing it into a thick batter, which will feel more like a cake-mixture than batter. Beat hard for several minutes. The mixture should be able to drop easily, but should not be too thin. Leave it for 10–15 minutes.

To make the syrup

Using a spacious saucepan, mix the sugar and water together, and boil fairly quickly for 8 minutes. Test by dropping a little of it on a plate – if it forms into a still ball then it is ready. Add the rest of the saffron and keep it by you, on the lowest possible heat.

To fry the boondi

Using a deep chip pan, put 225g (8oz) of the butter-fat in it (keeping 25g (1oz) for mixing-in afterwards), and bring to nearly smoking point. To test the temperature, it is best to fry one or two drops of mixture first. Using a turner or slice, place about a tablespoon of the mixture on it and tap the slice on the inside edges of the pan to make the mixture fall through the holes into the hot fat. This boondi should be fried fairly quickly and, as soon as one

125

batch is done, place it in the syrup. Keep moving the soaked boondi to the sides of the saucepan and, if the syrup is too dry, sprinkle a little hot water on it. When all the mixture has been used and the boondi is in the syrup, mix thoroughly with a slice and add the nuts and cardamom seeds.

Heat the remaining 25g (1oz) of butter-fat and pour it onto the mixture. When slightly cool, form into balls or laddoos by taking some of this mixed boondi, pressing it hard, then shaping it by moving it from one hand to the other and pressing hard all the time.

Laddoo boondi are a traditional Indian sweetmeat and are a great favourite with grown-ups and children alike. No Indian feast is complete without them.

Note: Saffron should be in the form of small fragments.

Semolina Laddoo

Laddoo Suji

100g (4oz) very fine semolina	*1 teaspoon cardamom seeds or*
100g (4oz) set butter-fat	*nutmeg*
100g (4oz) caster sugar	*1 tablespoon, or more, of finely*
	sliced almonds or other nuts

For 12–14 laddoos
Using a thick aluminium saucepan, fry the semolina in the butter-fat quite slowly for about 15 minutes. When the fat seems to separate from the semolina and the sweet fragrance starts to come from it, then it is ready. Care should be taken not to allow the semolina to become brown. Remove from the heat, cool slightly, add sugar and mix thoroughly with a spoon: add the cardamom seeds or nutmeg and the finely sliced nuts. Mix once more and, when the mixture is fairly cold, form into small balls or laddoos.

The above method is also used for laddoo besan.

Pinnis – made with Wholemeal Flour and Khoya

100g (4oz) wholemeal flour
100g (4oz) set butter-fat
175g (6oz) caster sugar
50g (2oz) khoya or full-cream
   powdered milk
1 tablespoon dessicated coconut

1–2 tablespoon finely sliced almonds
   or other nuts
1½ tablespoons sultanas
1 teaspoon crushed cardamom seeds
   or grated nutmeg

For 15–20 pinnis
Fry the flour in the butter-fat in the same way as in the previous recipe. Allow to cool slightly, then add the caster sugar and khoya or full-cream powdered milk. If full-cream powdered milk is used, it should be mixed with about 1½ tablespoons of water (hot) and beaten until it is like stiff pastry before mixing in with the fried flour and sugar. Add the nuts and sultanas, sprinkle with cardamom seeds or nutmeg and mix thoroughly. Form into pinnis of the desired size, which will keep for several days.

Pinnis are slightly flatter than laddoos.

Pinnis made with Dal or Lentil Mixture

1 teacup dal urad (see page 7)
   or red lentils
225g (8oz) butter-fat
275g (10oz) sugar (preferably
   caster)

2 tablespoons sliced pistachio
   or almond nuts
1½ tablespoons desiccated coconut
½–1 teaspoon separated cardamom
   seeds or grated nutmeg

For 20 pinnis
Soak the dal urad or lentils overnight, then drain them well and leave to dry slightly for a while. Then, using a pestle and mortar, crush and pound them, a little at a time, until they almost resemble cake mixture. Using an aluminium saucepan, fry this mixture fairly slowly in the butter-fat for 8–10 minutes. Remove from the heat, scrape from the sides and bottom, and continue stirring until it is half cold. Add sugar, nuts (saving some of them for decorating the top) and the cardamom seeds; mix thoroughly and leave until quite cold. Then, taking a little of the mixture, form each pinnis (slightly flatter than laddoos), and place in a shallow, buttered dish. Keep repeating the process until all the pinnis are formed, then decorate the top with sliced nuts. The pinnis will be set and ready to serve after an hour or so.

    These pinnis are considered very nourishing, and are especially recommended for convalescents.

A Syrupy Sweetmeat

Gulab Jamans

1.5 litres (2½ pints) milk
   (preferably full-fat)
1 tablespoon lemon juice
1 teaspoon plain or self-raising
   flour
2 dozen small pistachio kernels
   or almonds

1½ teacups sugar
1½ teacups water
175g–225g (6–8oz) of fat, for
   frying
1 tablespoon rosewater

For 18 gulab jamans

Make panir (soft milk 'cheese', see page 5) in the usual way by using 600ml (1 pint) of milk; make khoya (condensed milk, see page 5) with the remainder of the milk.

Mix the panir, khoya and flour together, pound and knead well until the mixture is smooth and feels like stiff pastry. Take a small portion of this pastry, shape it into a narrow sausage 3.5–5cm (1½–2in) long, break in half and place a very small nut, or part of one, in between, and then press and shape together again. Make as many gulab jamans this way as the mixture will furnish, and have them ready for cooking.

Put the sugar and water in a saucepan and boil quickly for seven minutes. When the syrup is sticky (not too stiff) leave it over a very low heat. Place the fat in a chip pan and, when it is hot (not quite smoking), fry the gulab jamans 4 or 5 at a time in the deep fat, quite slowly, turning them just once. When they have risen and are of almond brown colour, take them out of the fat, drain and place them in the warm syrup. Repeat the process until all are made. Remove from the heat and place the gulab jamans and syrup in a dish. When cool, add the rosewater.

Gulab jamans are served either warm or cold with a little of the syrup. They are a well-known Indian sweetmeat and a great favourite, either as an after-dinner sweet, or at tea time. They can be made entirely of khoya, instead of khoya and panir, the rest of the ingredients being the same.

Gulab Jaman, with Khoya and Potato Pastry

3 medium-sized potatoes (which
    should make 100g (4oz) potato
    pastry)
900ml (1½ pints) milk (preferably
    the 300ml (½ pint) to be
    full-fat milk)

1 tablespoon self-raising flour (not
    wholemeal)
½ teaspoon crushed cardamom
    seeds or grated nutmeg
1 tablespoon rosewater

For syrup, etc.

225g (½lb) sugar
1½ teacups water

225g (8oz) of fat, for frying

For 14 gulab jamans

Boil the potatoes in their jackets and, when cooked (not broken), cool and carefully skin them, then mash and knead. Using a thick aluminium frying pan, mix the milk and the potato pastry together, and boil fairly quickly for an hour, scraping frequently from the base and sides of the pan until the mixture is quite thick. Then stir vigorously and reduce the excess liquid. Remove from the heat and turn the mixture onto a plate. When slightly cold, mix in the flour and the crushed cardamom seeds or grated nutmeg.

Shape the gulab jamans in the same way as in the previous gulab jaman recipe, except that the pieces of nuts are not placed in the centre of each one.

To make the syrup

Using a large saucepan, mix the sugar and water together and boil quickly for 6–8 minutes. The syrup should be quite sticky, but not too stiff. Keep it warm over the lowest possible heat.

Fry the gulab jamans 3 or 4 at a time in deep, hot fat over rather less than medium heat, and not too slowly. When they are fairly brown on both sides, take them out and place them in the syrup. When all are done, bring the syrup to the boil with the gulab jamans in it. Care must be taken not to crush them; a slice or turner (not a spoon) should be used for shifting and turning them.

When slightly cool, put them – syrup and all – into a glass dish and add the rosewater. Serve warm or cold.

These gulab jamans are delicious and the addition of the potato pastry seems to make them tastier still.

Another Variety of Syrupy Sweetmeat

Rasgullas

1.7 litres (3 pints) milk
3 tablespoons slightly warm lemon
   juice, or 1½ teacups milk curd
1 dessertspoon very fine semolina
12 small pieces broken-up lump
   sugar

2 teacups sugar
4 teacups water
1½ tablespoons of rosewater for
   flavouring

To make panir (soft milk 'cheese')

For 10–12 rasgullas
Boil the milk, stirring continuously to prevent skin from forming on the top. As the milk comes up to the boil, add the slightly warmed lemon juice or curd, and bring to the boil. When solid lumps have formed, strain off through a muslin bag, place the bag on a clean board and press with fairly heavy weight to get rid of all the liquid.

To prepare rasgullas

Empty the panir onto a clean board, add fine semolina, and pound and knead until it starts to become greasy. From this, form 12 round balls. Break each ball in half and place a small piece of sugar between, then press and shape them together again.

To make the syrup
Mix the sugar and water together, boil for seven minutes over medium heat. Take out 1½ teacups of this thin syrup and keep it by you.

Place the rasgullas into the syrup remaining in the saucepan, bring quickly to the boil, then turn heat down low and keep boiling gently (uncovered), shaking the saucepan frequently. Gradually add the syrup previous removed, so that the rasgullas are being cooked in *thin* syrup all the time. This will take about an hour and a quarter and, when ready, the rasgullas should be quite swollen and the syrup should be white in appearance. Remove from the heat and after partly cooling, add the rosewater.

Rasgullas are served warm or cold, with a little of the syrup. They are a well-known Indian sweetmeat and a great favourite, either as an after-dinner sweet or at tea time. Some people pour some cream or rabri (see page 21) over them before serving.

Curly Sweetmeat

Jalebis

1½ teacups plain flour
2 tablespoons milk-curd
1 teacups warm water

1 teaspoon saffron (optional)
600 ml (1 pint) of oil or fat for
   frying
A medium-sized heat-proof funnel

For syrup

2 teacups sugar

2 teacups water

For 18 jalebis

Sieve the flour into a basin and, by gradually adding the curd and water, make it into a thick batter. Add the saffron (if using), and beat hard for several minutes. Let this stand overnight in a warm place.

Make the syrup by boiling the sugar and water together over a medium heat for 7–10 minutes. The syrup should be quite sticky but not stiff, and should be kept at a tepid temperature before use.

Heat the fat in a deep frying pan to nearly smoking point, then fill a heat proof funnel with the well-beaten batter. Finger and shape each jalebi as the batter pours into the fat by moving the funnel around 3 or 4 times at one place in the pan to make a curly ring about the size of a small pineapple ring. Fry three or four jalebis at a time and, when golden brown on both sides, drain on a slice with holes in it, and dip in the syrup. When they have soaked up sufficient syrup, place the jalebis in a row in a large, shallow dish.

Jalebis are a well-known Indian sweetmeat and can be served hot or cold. Some people like them soaked in milk.

INDIAN cooking

Sweetmeat made with Soft Milk Cheese

Sandesh

1.7 litres (3 pints) fresh milk
3 tablespoons lemon juice, or
   1½ teacups milk-curd
200g (7oz) sugar

2 dozen or more pistachio kernels
   or other nuts
1 teaspoon, or more, crushed
   cardamom seeds or grated nutmeg

For 10 or 12 pieces
Heat the milk in a heavy saucepan and, when it comes to the boil, add the lemon juice or the milk-curd. Keep over a low heat for a minute or two, and stir until solid lumps are formed. Strain into a muslin bag and, leaving it on a board, press with heavy weight for 15 minutes or longer. Shred the panir into a heavy aluminium saucepan, add sugar and place over a low heat. Stir well for 10 minutes or so. It will loosen at first and then thicken up. When fairly thick, remove from the heat and turn the mixture into small diamond-shaped tins. Decorate each one with finely-sliced kernels and the crushed cardamom seeds or grated nutmeg. When thoroughly cold, remove them carefully from the tins.

If tins are not available, spread the mixture thickly on a shallow plate and decorate. When half-cold, cut into diamond-shaped pieces, but do not separate them until they are almost cold.

This sweetmeat is very delicious and quite easy to make.

Mysore Sweetmeat

Masur Pak I

1–2 tablespoons sliced almonds
1 teaspoon crushed cardamom
    seeds or any other sweet
    flavouring
1 dessertspoon ground almonds
175g (6oz) butter-fat, clarified
    margarine, or a mixture of the two

2 heaped tablespoons besan or
    fine split-pea flour*
225g (8oz) sugar
½ teacup water

For 15 pieces
Keep near you the sliced almonds, crushed cardamom seeds and the ground almonds. Take out nearly 50g (2oz) butter-fat, warm it and keep it to use later on. Place the rest of the butter-fat or margarine-fat in a thick aluminium frying pan, and let it melt.

Sieve the flour and gradually add it to the simmering fat. Fry gently for 4–5 minutes, then add the ground almonds and the flavouring. Keep it over a very low heat. Mix the sugar and water together and boil for 4 minutes over medium heat, by which time the syrup should be quite sticky. Pour this over the frying flour: mix quickly, and fry over medium heat for 7–8 minutes, adding a dessertspoon of warm butter-fat after every 2 minutes, and stirring continuously. The mixture then should be quite thick and of a slightly spongy appearance. Spread it thickly in a shallow dish and decorate it soon afterwards, because this mixture dries very quickly.

When half cold, carefully cut into diamond-shaped pieces.

This sweetmeat is also a well-known one, and very easy to make.

* Plain Flour (not wholemeal) can be used in place of besan or split-pea flour.

Masur Pak II

175g (6oz) butter-fat, clarified
  margarine, or a mixture of the
  two
225g (8oz) sugar
1 teacup water
2 heaped tablespoons besan or
  fine split-pea flour

1 dessertspoon ground almonds
1–2 tablespoons sliced almonds
1 teaspoon crushed cadarmom seeds
  or any other sweet flavouring

For 15 pieces
Place the butter-fat, sugar and water in a heavy frying pan. Boil these over
medium heat for about 8 minutes. Turn the heat down lower and in this
sizzling mixture, mix the well-sieved besan flour little by little, and stir
vigorously. Add the ground almonds. Keep stirring for 5–6 minutes, when the
mixture should be fairly thick and spongy.

Spread thickly on a dish, decorate with sliced almonds and crushed
cardamom seeds or other sweet flavouring, and soon afterwards cut
carefully into desired pieces.

Condensed Milk Sweetmeat

Sohan Halva

100g (4oz) khoya (home-made
   condensed milk) (see page 5)
   or khoya made with powdered
   milk
100g (4oz) butter-fat

175g (6oz) sugar
1–2 tablespoons sliced mixed nuts
1–2 dozen pistachio or almond nuts
1 teaspoon crushed cardamom
   seeds or grated nutmeg

Will make 12 squares

Place the khoya in a thick aluminium saucepan. Add 75g (3oz) of butter-fat, and let it cook gently for 4–5 minutes, stirring frequently. Add the sugar, stir vigorously, keeping the heat at medium until the mixture is fairly thick, which should not take more than 10 minutes. Remove from the heat, and spread the mixture on a buttered dish, and decorate with sliced nuts, pistachio or almond nuts and cardamom seeds or nutmeg. Heat the remainder of the butter-fat and pour this over the top. Leave to cool and then cut into pieces of the desired size.

   This is a very delicious sweetmeat and it will retain its flavour for several weeks, particularly if it is made with home-made condensed milk khoya.

Carrot Sweetmeat

900ml (1½ pints) fresh milk
100g (¼lb) freshly grated carrots
150g (5oz) sugar
2 tablespoons set butter-fat
2 tablespoons well-washed sultanas
   (optional)

1 teaspoon desiccated coconut
2 tablespoons finely sliced mixed
   nuts
1 teaspoon crushed cardamom seeds
   or grated nutmeg

For 15 squares
Using a large, heavy aluminium frying pan, put the milk and grated carrots to boil on medium heat. Keep boiling until the mixture thickens, stirring frequently. This should take about 45 minutes. Add sugar and keep stirring for another 15 minutes, then add the butter-fat. Turn the heat a little lower, and keep frying and mixing until most of the fat has been absorbed in the mixture: this should take less than ten minutes. Add the sultanas and mix thoroughly. Remove from heat, and pour the sweetmeat onto a shallow, buttered dish. Spread it thickly, and decorate with desiccated coconut, mixed nuts and the crushed cardamom seeds.

When cool, cut into pieces of the desired size.

This sweetmeat is very tasty and nourishing.

Almond Sweetmeat with Full-cream Powdered Milk

450ml (¾ pint) fresh milk
40g (1½oz) ground almonds
2 dozen almond nuts
150g (5oz) sugar

50g (2oz) full-cream powdered milk
1 teaspoon crushed cardamom
 seeds or grated nutmeg

For 15 small pieces
Using a heavy aluminium frying pan, boil the fresh milk; add the ground almonds and boil fairly quickly until the mixture thickens. This should not take more than 20 minutes. Add the powdered milk and cook gently for 5–7 minutes. Then add the sugar, mix well and keep over medium heat for another 10 minutes. The mixture should now be fairly thick. Remove and spread out evenly into a well-buttered shallow dish.

Decorate with peeled and sliced almonds and cardamom seeds or nutmeg. Cut into shapes when almost cold.

Coconut Sweetmeat I

900ml (1½ pints) milk
1 dessertspoon coarse desiccated
   coconut or fresh grated coconut
225g (½lb) sugar
1 teacup finely desiccated coconut

1 teaspoon crushed cardamom
   seeds or grated nutmeg
A few pieces of edible silver
   leaf or silver balls

For 16–18 squares
Boil the milk in a heavy aluminium frying pan, mix in the coconut and boil for just over 30 minutes, when the mixture should be quite thick. Add sugar, and keep cooking and stirring for another 10–15 minutes until there is no excess milk left in the sweetmeat. Pour into a well buttered dish and decorate with the coarse desiccated coconut, cardamom seeds and the strips of edible silver leaf (or silver balls). Cut into shapes when almost cold.

Coconut Sweetmeat II with Full-cream Powdered Milk

225g (½ pint) full-fat milk
50g (2oz) full-cream powdered milk
½ teacup fine desiccated coconut
1 dessertspoon crushed walnuts
   or sliced coconut

150g (5oz) sugar
1 teaspoon crushed cardamom seeds
   or grated nutmeg

For 16–18 squares
Put the milk and coconut in a heavy aluminium frying pan, and boil fairly quickly until all the excess milk has dried out. Prepare the mock khoya by the usual method (see page 5) and place it in the frying mixture, mix and fry for another five minutes. Then add sugar, stir well and fry over medium heat until the mixture is fairly dry – this should not take more than 10 minutes. Transfer to a shallow, buttered dish and decorate with nuts and cardamom seeds.

Cut into pieces of the desired size when half-cold.

Barphi I with Condensed Milk

100g (4oz) khoya (home-made
  condensed milk out of
  900ml/1½ pints)
100g (4oz) sugar
1 tablespoon ground almonds
  (optional)

Butter-fat for greasing
1 teaspoon cardamom seeds
1 dozen pistachio nuts (finely sliced)
Some silver leaf for decorating

For 12 pieces
Make the khoya by boiling 900ml (1½ pints) fresh milk until it is very thick.
If you use a heavy aluminium frying pan, the condensing should not take
more than an hour. Set aside and allow to cool. Then place the khoya and
sugar in a heavy aluminium saucepan, and mix and cook very gently for
nearly 10 minutes, taking care not to let the mixture stick to the bottom. Mix
in the ground almonds (if using), and transfer the mixture to a shallow dish
that has been well greased with butter-fat. When slightly cool, pat and
spread with the palm of the hand and decorate with the crushed cardamom
seeds, pistachio nuts and silver leaf. Cut slantwise into diamond shapes.

Barphi II with Full-cream Powdered Milk

225g (8oz) sugar
1 teacup water
100g (4oz) full-cream powdered
   milk

1 teaspoon crushed cardamom seeds
1 dozen pistachio nuts (finely sliced)
Edible silver leaf or balls

For 20 pieces
Boil the sugar and water fairly quickly for 6 or 7 minutes. The syrup should then be so thick that a little of it dropped onto a plate forms a round ball. Then add the powdered milk; mix well and then turn the mixture onto a well-greased shallow plate. Pat and spread with the palm of your hands, and cut the mixture slantwise into diamond shapes.

   Decorate with crushed cardamom seeds, pistachio nuts and the silver leaf or balls.

INDIAN cooking

Sweetmeat with Condensed Milk

Peras

100g (4oz) khoya (home-made
    condensed milk from
    900ml/1½ pints milk)
1 teaspoon set butter-fat

100g (4oz) sugar (preferably caster)
1½ dozen pistachio nuts
1 teaspoon crushed cardamom
    seeds or grated nutmeg

For 10 peras
Make the khoya by boiling 900ml (1½ pints) of milk in a heavy aluminium frying pan and allowing it to cool. Warm the butter-fat in a heavy aluminium saucepan over a low heat.

Rub the khoya in your hands and break up any lumps, and put it into the saucepan. Stir and mix for 4–5 minutes, still keeping over very low heat. Add sugar and mix again for 3 minutes. When the sugar is warmed through and well mixed, remove the mixture from the heat and beat with a spoon for several minutes. When it is smooth and pliable, take a small portion and, using the palm of your hand, shape it into a round biscuit (not too thin). Make each one separately, and place on a shallow dish that has been well greased with butter-fat. Decorate them with the finely sliced pistachio nuts and crushed cardamom seeds or grated nutmeg. When shaping the peras, if the mixture is slightly sticky, it is permissible to use a little more of the caster sugar as you go along, but the mixture should not be allowed to get 'loose'.

Sugar-coated Sweetmeat

Balu Shai

225g (½lb) plain flour (not
   wholemeal)
75g (3oz) set butter-fat
1 teaspoon baking powder

1½ tablespoons milk-curd or warm
   milk
1 tablespoon warm water
225g (½lb) fat for frying

For syrup

275g (10oz) sugar

1½ teacups water

For 18 balu shais

Sieve the flour in a mixing bowl, add the well-heated butter-fat and the baking powder. Rub the mixture with your hands, gradually adding the milk-curd and warm water, and mix into a stiff dough. Break off a small portion of the dough, roll it into a ball, then flatten it so that it resembles a small, round thick shortbread and make a deep dent in the centre. Shape all the balu shais by this method.

    To prepare the syrup, boil the sugar and water together in a large saucepan fairly quickly for 7–10 minutes: the syrup should be quite sticky. Keep this warm over a very low heat. Heat the frying fat in a chip pan, and fry the balu shais quite slowly until they are golden brown, and when they are done, put them in the warm syrup. When all are fried, let them simmer in the warm syrup for a few minutes, shaking the pan frequently to let them become well-coated with syrup. Take them out singly from the pan and place on a shallow dish. Serve cold at tea time.

INDIAN cooking

Sugar-coated cubes

Shakar Pare

1 teacup plain flour (not wholemeal)
1 tablespoon set butter-fat
1 dessertspoon ground almonds

1–1½ tablespoon milk-curd or milk
Some oil or fat for frying

For syrup

1 teacup sugar

1 teacup water

For 26 pieces

Sieve the flour into a mixing bowl. Heat the butter-fat until smoking hot and pour it onto the flour. Add the ground almonds, mix well and gradually add the heated-up milk-curd or milk. Knead this for several minutes, make the whole mixture into a smooth ball shape, then roll it out a little less than 1cm (½ins) thick. Cut into 2.5cm (1in) long cubes. Heat the oil or fat in a deep chip pan and bring carefully to nearly smoking point. Carefully put in a handful of cubes at a time and fry very gently until the shakar pare are of almond-skin colour. Drain, and put them straight into the syrup (which has been prepared beforehand by mixing the sugar and water together and boiling fairly quickly in a large saucepan for 7–8 minutes). When one batch has been dipped in the syrup, they should be taken out and placed on a shallow dish. When all are done, pour the remainder of the syrup over the lot, so that they get well-coated in sugar. When cold, they will be inclined to stick together a little, but they can be easily separated. Some of the dried sugar which remains at the bottom of the dish can be scraped off and put away for another use.

Shakar pare are a traditional sweetmeat and are served with other sweetmeats at marriage feasts.

Stuffed Sweet Samosas

50g (2oz) plain flour
15g (½oz) butter-fat
About 1 tablespoon hot water
Dry flour for rolling out

Warm water or milk
Some fat or oil for frying
1 tablespoon sliced pistachio nuts
   for decorating

For stuffing

50g (2oz) khoya (see page 5)
   or mock khoya
1 tablespoon sultanas

25g (1oz) sugar
1–2 dozen chopped or ground
   almonds
½ teaspoon crushed cardamom seeds

For syrup

100g (4oz) sugar

½ teacup water

For 8 samosas
Sieve the flour in a mixing bowl, add 15g (½oz) of butter-fat, rub it in with
your hands and, by gradually adding the hot water, mix all into a stiff pastry.

To prepare the stuffing

Knead 50g (2oz) khoya (if mock khoya is being used, it should be prepared
in advance by mixing 1½ tablespoons water in 50g (2oz) dried milk). Add
well washed, soaked and drained sultanas, chopped or ground nuts, sugar
and the cardamom seeds, and mix well.

To make the syrup

Boil the sugar and water together fairly quickly for 3–4 minutes. The syrup
should be quite sticky, but not stiff. Keep it slightly warm.

To shape samosas

Take a small portion of the pastry, shape into a ball, roll it out with the help of a little dry flour as thin and round as possible. Cut this pancake in half, take one semi-circle piece in your hand, place 1 tablespoon of stuffing on one half of this piece, leaving the edges free, which should then be wetted with warm water or milk. Now fold over the unfilled half on top of the other and tightly close the edges together forming a three-cornered stuffed cushion shape. Continue the process until all the samosas are ready.

To fry the samosas

Heat the fat or oil in a chip pan and fry the samosas singly and quite slowly. After frying, dip each one in syrup, and place in a shallow dish. The tops of the samosas can be decorated with the sliced pistachio nuts. Some of the oil and syrup will be left over and can be used again.

   The stuffing for the sweet samosas can be made out of 50g (2oz) of ground almonds instead of khoya or mock khoya. The ground almonds should be mixed in a little cream, then sugar, sultanas and crushed cardamom seeds or grated nutmeg added to them.

INDIAN cooking

Tea-time Savouries

Savoury Cakes

Matthies (Mathris)

3 teacups plain flour (not
   wholemeal)
2½ tablespoons set butter-fat
1½–2 teaspoons salt
1 dessertspoon caraway seeds
   (optional)

About 2 tablespoons hot water
2 tablespoons milk-curd or milk
600ml (1 pint) liquid fat or frying oil

For 27 matthies

Sieve the flour into a mixing bowl; heat the butter-fat to nearly smoking point and pour it onto the flour. Add salt and caraway seeds (if using), and mix well with your hands, gradually adding the hot water and milk-curd. The pastry for matthies should be quite stiff and well worked. Take a small piece of pastry and, after making a ball of it, roll it out into the shape of a large, round biscuit (not too thin). Due to the stiffness of the pastry, the edges will be uneven.

Put the liquid fat or oil in a deep frying pan and bring it to nearly smoking point. Fry the matthies quite slowly, putting 3 or 4 in the pan at a time, turning with a slice whenever necessary. They should not be allowed to get really brown.

Small triangular-shaped or cube-shaped cakes can also be made. For the former, after shaping the piece of pastry into a ball, roll out into a small thin pancake, cut in half and then fold twice into a triangular shape.

For a cube shape, roll a lump of pastry out in the same way as for biscuits and cut into the desired shape.

Matthies are usually served cold and are a great tea time favourite. In an airtight tin, they will keep for nearly a fortnight.

INDIAN cooking

Savoury Vegetable Fritters

Pakoras

For the batter

1½ teacups besan (split-pea flour)
About 1 teacup water
2 teaspoons salt
½ teaspoon turmeric

1 teaspoon garam-masala
½ teaspoon chilli powder
1 tablespoon pomegranate seeds

For vegetables, etc.

1 large potato
1 large onion, peeled
100g (¼lb) cauliflower
A few pieces of marrow or some
   spinach

1½ teaspoons salt
½ teaspoon garam-masala
½ teaspoon chilli powder
About 600ml (1 pint) oil or the
   equivalent of fat for frying

To make the batter

For 20–30 pakoras
Sieve the flour in a mixing bowl and gradually add the water. First, make it as stiff as dough then, by continually adding a little more water and beating hard all the time; bring it to the consistency of thick batter and then leave for 30 minutes. Add salt, turmeric, garam-masala, chilli powder and pomegranate seeds. Beat once again for several minutes, keeping the batter fairly thick.

Tea-time Savouries

To prepare the vegetables

Scrape, wash and cut the potato into thin, round slices and do the same with the onion. The pieces of cauliflower and marrow should be fairly thin and about 3.5cm (1½in) long. Drain the vegetables well and mix salt, garam-masala and chilli powder with them.

To fry the pakoras

Using a deep frying pan, bring the oil or fat to nearly smoking point. Coat each piece of vegetable separately with the batter and drop it into the hot fat. Fry as many pakorhas at a time as the pan will conveniently hold, over medium heat and not too quickly. Turn them frequently and, when golden brown all round, drain well and remove from the pan.

Pakoras are crisper if they are allowed to cool for a little while after frying, and then fried once again quickly before serving.

Besides the vegetables mentioned above, the following can also be used for pakoras: spinach, aubergines, green chillis and red peppers.

Some people mix vegetables, cut them small, wrap them in batter and fry them instead of picking each one separately.

Potatos can be boiled in their jackets, skinned and mashed well, and seasoned, and are then made into small flat cakes, coated well with the batter, and fried as ordinary pakorhas.

Pakoras are a well-known Indian savoury delicacy and are served hot or warm at tea time with some mint or tamarind chutney.

INDIAN cooking

Triangular Cakes, stuffed with Potato

Samosa Alu

For the stuffing

2 fairly large potatoes
1 small onion, peeled
2 tablespoons broken-up coriander
  or other herbs
A small piece of ginger, and
  ½ teaspoon chilli powder
  (optional)

1 dessertspoon butter-fat
1½ teaspoons salt
1 teaspoon garam-masala
1 tablespoon ground mango, or
  1 dessertspoon lemon juice
1 tablespoon dried pomegranate
  seeds

For pastry, etc.

1 teacup plain flour (not
  wholemeal)
1 dessertspoon butter-fat
½ teaspoon salt

2 tablespoons, or more, milk-curd,
  or warm milk, for mixing
Dry flour, for rolling out
Some oil or fat for frying

To prepare pastry for samosas

For 14 samosas
Sieve the flour in a mixing bowl, heat the butter-fat and pour it onto the flour. Add salt and mix into a stiff pastry by gradually adding the milk-curd or warm milk.

Tea-time Savouries

For the stuffing

Boil the potatoes in their jackets: when cool, peel and mash them. Mince or finely chop the onion, herbs and ginger (if using). Heat the butter-fat in a frying pan and fry the onion mixture in it very gently for 2 or 3 minutes. Add the prepared potatoes, salt, garam-masala, chilli powder (if using), ground mango or lemon juice and the pomegranate seeds. Mix well and keep over the heat for a short while until the mixture is well dry, then remove from the heat and keep by for stuffing the samosas.

To shape the samosas

Break off a little of the pastry, shape it into a ball, roll it out with the help of a little dry flour as thin and round as possible. Cut this pancake in half, hold one semicircle in your hand, place about 1 tablespoon of the potato mixture on one half of this piece, leaving the edges free, which should then be pasted inside and out with the milk-curd or milk. Now fold over the unfilled half on top of the other and tightly close the edges together.

Heat the oil or fat in a deep frying pan or chip pan. When smoking hot, fry the prepared samosas in it, 2 at a time, fairly slowly. When golden brown on both sides, drain well and remove from pan.

Samosas are usually served hot, with mint or tamarind chutney, at tea time. They are a great favourite with grown-ups and children alike.

Samosas stuffed with Peas and Potato

For stuffing

3 medium-sized potatoes
1 dessertspoon set butter-fat
1 medium-sized onion, peeled
A small piece of ginger
7g (¼oz) coriander or other herbs
1 teaspoon salt
½ teaspoon (or more) chilli
    powder (optional)

2 small tomatoes
1 teacup freshly shelled peas
1 teaspoon garam-masala
1 dessertspoon ground mango or
    lemon juice
Milk-curd for brushing pastry

For pastry, etc.

1 teacup plain flour (not wholemeal)
1 dessertspoon set butter-fat
Some oil or fat for frying

½ teaspoon salt
2 tablespoons (or a little more)
    milk-curd or warm milk for mixing

To prepare the stuffing

For 14 samosas
Boil the potatoes in their jackets. When tender, let cool, skin them and dice into very small cubes. Using a deep frying pan, fry in the butter-fat the minced onions, ginger (if root ginger is used, it should be soaked first) and the herbs. Add salt, chilli powder (if using) and sliced tomatoes. Stir well and allow to sizzle for a few minutes. Put in the peas, mix and cook gently (covered) for 10 minutes. Next, mix in the diced potatoes, add garam-masala and ground mango or lemon juice, and cook until fairly dry before removing from the heat.

Prepare the pastry as in previous recipe (page 154-5) and shape, stuff and fry the samosas as before. The pea and potato stuffing is inclined to open the edges of the samosas, so the inside and outside edges of each samosa should be slightly pasted with milk-curd before sticking together and frying.

Samosa Stuffed with Meat

For stuffing

1 medium-sized onion, peeled
A small piece of ginger, and ½
    teaspoon chilli powder (optional)
1 large red pepper, chopped or
    7g (¼oz) fresh herbs
1 dessertspoon butter-fat
½ teaspoon turmeric

1 teaspoon salt
1 large tomato
175g (6oz) lean minced meat
1 teacup hot water
½–1 teaspoon garam-masala
1 tablespoon ground mango, or
    1 dessertspoon lemon juice

For pastry

1 teacup plain flour (not wholemeal)
1 dessertspoon set butter-fat
½ teaspoon salt

2 tablespoons milk-curd or warm
    milk for mixing
Some oil or fat for frying

For 14 samosas
Prepare the pastry in the same manner as for other samosas (see pages154-5).
    For the stuffing, gently fry the minced onions, ginger (if using) and pepper or herbs together in the hot butter-fat. Add turmeric, salt and chilli powder (if using). Fry for 2–3 minutes, then add the sliced tomatoes. Mix well, then put in the minced meat. Let it sizzle for 5 minutes, then pour the hot water on it. Bring to the boil, then turn the heat down very low, and cook for about 45 minutes. Add garam-masala and the ground mango or lemon juice. Slightly mash the meat which should now be well cooked and dry. Allow to cool. Then stuff the samosas with the meat in the usual way. Paste the edges of samosas (inside and out) with the milk-curd or warm milk, close them properly, and fry in the hot oil or fat, as before.

INDIAN cooking

Savoury Drops

Namkin Boondi

2 teacups besan (split-pea flour)
1½ teaspoons salt
½ teaspoon garam-masala
½ teaspoon chilli powder (optional)
1 tablespoon butter-fat

½ teacup (or little more) warm water
Some oil or fat for frying
½–1 teaspoon ajvayn seeds (optional)
½ teaspoon turmeric

For 6 or 7 people
Sieve the flour into a mixing bowl, add salt, garam-masala, turmeric, ajvayn seeds and chilli powder (if using). Heat the butter-fat to boiling point, pour it on the flour and mix well. Add the warm water gradually (split-pea flour will need a little more water), beating the mixture thoroughly as if making a sponge mixture: the more beating, the crisper the boondi will be. The texture should be like a thin, smooth cake mixture rather than batter. Heat the frying oil or fat in a large, deep frying pan or chip pan: place a large spoonful of the mixture onto a large, round slice or turner with medium-sized holes. With the laden slice in your right hand and firmly gripping the handle of the frying pan with the other, tap the slice against the inner edges of the pan so that the boondi mixture falls into the smoking fat in droplets (not too much of the mixture at a time). Some of the boondi may be inclined to stick together, but they can easily be separated with your fingers after they have been fried. Frying should be done over a medium heat, and boondi should be golden brown all over and well drained before they are taken from the pan. Repeat the process until all the mixture has been used. Remove the boondi onto another large shallow dish so that no excess fat is left on them.

When thoroughly cold, they should be kept in a tin. Namkin boondi is usually served cold at tea time and is a great favourite.

Savoury Saivia (Sivaiya)

2 teacups besan, or very fine
   split-pea flour
2 teaspoons salt
¼ teaspoon turmeric
1 teaspoon chilli powder (optional)

1 teaspoon ajvayn seeds, or any
   other savoury flavouring
1½ tablespoons set butter-fat
About ½ teacup warm water for mixing
Some oil or fat for frying

Sieve the flour into a mixing bowl, add the salt and the rest of the ingredients, followed by the heated-up butter-fat. Rub well with your hands, and make it into a stiff dough by gradually adding the warm water. Knead for a few minutes.

   Heat the deep fat or oil in a chip pan, place the dough in a clean pasta-machine or electric mouli-shredder fitted with the finest gauge, and pass the dough through to form thin strips directly over the hot oil or fat. Fry slowly in the near-smoking oil or fat, repeating the process until all the dough is used up.

   Savoury saivia are very tasty, crisp and crunchy, and are served at tea time.

INDIAN cooking

Similar to Potato Rissoles

Alu Tikia

450g (1lb) potatoes
1½ teaspoons salt
1 teaspoon garam-masala
7g (¼oz) finely chopped ginger,
 and ½ teaspoon chilli powder,
 or 2 chopped fresh green
 chillies (optional)
1–2 tablespoons broken-up
 coriander or other fresh herbs

1 egg, beaten
1 teaspoon set butter-fat
1 teacup freshly shelled peas
4 spring onions, peeled
1 dessertspoon lemon juice
Some oil or fat for frying

For 12 tikia
Prepare the potato pastry by the same method as given for potato koftas
(see page 64) and beat the egg.
 Heat the butter-fat in a small saucepan, wash the peas and put them in
the saucepan. Sprinkle a little salt and water on them, cover and allow to
simmer until tender, which should not take more than 6–7 minutes. Remove
from the heat and, when slightly cold, crush them a little and mix them in the
potato pastry. Add minced spring onion, ginger (if using), herbs, the
remainder of the salt, garam-masala, chopped fresh chillies or chilli powder,
and the lemon juice. Mix thoroughly and shape the tikia like thin, round
rissoles. Fry them in shallow, hot fat over medium heat, after dipping them
in the egg mixture.
 Serve hot or cold at any meal with chutney.

Savoury Potato Straws

Alu Lachche

2 medium-sized potatoes
Some fat or oil for frying
1 teaspoon salt

1 teaspoon ground caraway seeds
1 dessertspoon ground mango, and
   ½ teaspoon chilli powder
   (optional)

Scrape, wash and grate the potatoes; place in a colander and wash them again under running water. Drain and dry them well in a teacloth. All this has to be done fairly quickly. Using a chip pan, bring the deep fat or oil to smoking point, then fry the straws a handful at a time over medium heat.

When the straws are of a golden brown colour, take them out of the pan using a large slice with very small holes in it and, after draining off the fat, place them in a shallow dish.

When all are done, shift them onto another dish and mix in with them the rest of the ingredients.

Alu lachche are very tasty, and are usually served at tea time.

INDIAN cooking

Savoury Cubes

Namak Pare

1 teacup plain flour (not wholemeal)
1 tablespoon set butter-fat
¾ teaspoon salt
1 teaspoon caraway or ajvayn
   seeds (optional)

1–1½ tablespoons milk-curd or
   water
Some oil or fat for frying

Sieve the flour into a mixing bowl. Heat the butter-fat to smoking point and pour this onto the flour. Add salt and the ajowan or caraway seeds (if using), mix well, and gradually add the heated curd or water. Knead for several minutes; shape the whole of the pastry into a ball, and roll out on a bread-board to about 1cm (½in) thickness.

Heat the oil or fat, then cut the pastry into cubes of the desired size, and fry a handful at a time, quite slowly, until they are the colour of almond skin.

Namak pare are served cold at tea time, or with cold drinks.

Channa Dal or Split Peas (Fried)

1 tablespoon bicarbonate of soda
1 teacup channa dal (see
   page 7)
Some oil or fat for frying
1 teaspoon salt

½ teaspoon garam-masala
¼ teaspoon chilli powder and
   1 dessertspoon ground mango
   (optional)

Soak the split peas in plenty of water, to which the bicarbonate of soda has been added. After soaking for 18 hours, take them out and soak them again for another 12 hours in fresh water. Then drain well and spread out on a clean cloth to dry, for at least an hour. Heat the oil or fat in a heavy chip pan over medium heat and, when smoking hot, fry a handful of split peas at a time, keeping over medium heat all the time. When they float on the top, allow a little more frying, and then take them out with a large round slice which has small holes. Drain well, and spread onto a shallow plate or tray.

When all the channa dal is fried, place on a clean cloth and wipe off as much of the oil as possible. When partially cool, coat them with the salt, garam-masala, chilli powder and ground mango (if using) mixed together.

Fried channa dal is crisp and very tasty, and is usually served at tea time.

Dal urad (see page 7) can also be fried by the same method, but reduce the soaking time to 18 hours.

INDIAN cooking

Semolina Shortbreads

Nan-Khatai

100g (4oz) set butter-fat
100g (4oz) sugar
175g (6oz) semolina
50g (2oz) plain or self-raising
  flour (not wholemeal)

1 teaspoon crushed cardamom
  seeds, or grated nutmeg
1 dozen or more pistachio kernels
  or almond nuts

For 22 shortbreads
Beat the butter-fat and sugar together for several minutes until the mixture is almost like cream. Gradually add the already sieved semolina and flour. Mix and beat once again and add the crushed cardamom seeds or nutmeg. No liquid is required.

Leave the mixture for 30 minutes or so, then knead well with your hands until it is very smooth to handle. Take a little of it, shape it into a small round shortcake and place it on a well-greased tin. Repeat until all the nan-khatais are prepared. Decorate with finely sliced kernels or nuts and bake them in a pre-heated oven (190°C/375°F/Gas 5) until they are a nice almond colour, which should take about half an hour.

When thoroughly cool, store in a tin.

Semolina Fried Cakes

Suji Karkarias

100g (4oz) semolina
600ml (1 pint) milk
1 tablespoon set butter-fat
150g (5oz) sugar
2 eggs

1 teaspoon crushed cardamoms or
    nutmeg, or other sweet flavouring
225g (½lb) of fat, for frying
1 tablespoon ground almonds

For 16 small cakes
Using an aluminium saucepan, mix the semolina in a little milk, then gradually add the rest of the milk. After adding the butter-fat and sugar, boil this mixture slowly until it is fairly thick, stirring all the time. Remove from the heat and allow to cool.

Beat the eggs and mix in the cold semolina mixture. Add the ground almonds, crushed cardamoms or grated nutmeg, and mix thoroughly.

Heat the fat in a deep chip pan to nearly smoking point. Take a dessertspoon of the mixture and fry it in the fat. Several spoonfuls can be fried at a time. When golden brown on both sides, drain and remove from the pan. Repeat the process until all the mixture is finished.

These cakes are crunchy and tasty, and are served cold at tea time.

INDIAN cooking

Gol Gappas

(These are small, round, hollow wafers, filled with savoury juice, or other stuffing)

For wafers

1 teacup plain flour (not wholemeal)
½ teaspoon, or less, of salt

½ teacup warm water
Some oil or fat for frying

For savoury juice

50g (2oz) tamarind or ground
    mango, or 2 tablespoons
    lemon juice
600ml (1 pint) water
2 tablespoons chopped mint

½ teaspoon chilli powder (optional)
1–2 teaspoons caraway seeds
½ teaspoon garam-masala
1 teaspoon salt
A pinch of ground ginger

To make savoury juice

For 40 wafers
Rinse and soak the tamarinds or mango in half the water for 15 minutes, then rub the fruit with your fingers so that the pulp comes away from the stones. Add the rest of the water, mix and strain through a strainer (not too fine), and throw away the stones and fibres. Add the rest of the ingredients, all finely ground and chopped, to this tamarind juice: mix well and leave for 2 hours. To save time, the savoury juice may be prepared by just mixing all the ingredients together and boiling them for 5–7 minutes, then letting the juice get thoroughly cold before serving.

Tea time Savouries

To make gol gappas

Sieve the flour in a mixing bowl, add salt, and first make it into a very stiff pastry by adding as little water as possible. Knead hard for several minutes and keep adding a little more water until you have used up about ½ teacup. Knead once again, then taking some of this pastry, make it into a round ball and, with the help of a little dry flour, roll it out as thinly as you can. Cut out quite small, round biscuit-shaped pieces, and fry them in deep fat over medium heat, 2 or 3 at a time. They should rise like balloons. Continue turning them and, when they are well cooked and brown, drain and place them in a shallow dish.

Gol gappas are served cold and are eaten filled with the savoury juice, which is added after making a hole in the centre of each gol gappa.

They may also be eaten filled with cooked kabli channas (page 91); potato chat (page 168); or dahi pakori (page 118).

INDIAN cooking

Potato Discs

Alu Chat

450g (1lb) potatoes (preferably
 small)
1½ teaspoons salt
½ teaspoon ground caraway seeds

2 tablespoons lemon juice
2 small chopped green chillies, or ½
 teaspoon chilli powder (optional)
½ teaspoon garam-masala

For 30 pieces
Scrub and boil the potatoes in their jackets. When cool, peel and slice them
into small, round pieces. Place in a shallow dish, and mix the rest of the
ingredients in them.

Alu chat is very tasty served in salad.

Instead of lemon juice, the pulp of 40g (1½oz) of tamarinds can be used,
which can be prepared by soaking the tamarinds in half a teacup of water,
and working the pulp away from the stones with your fingers.

Sweet potato chat and mixed fruit chat can be prepared the same way.

The fruits, such as bananas, apples, pears, plums, etc., are cut into small
pieces, mixed together and then salt, garam-masala, ground caraway seeds,
chopped green chillies or chilli powder are mixed in with them.

Chats are usually eaten with small sticks, similar to the ones used for
cocktail cherries.

INDIAN cooking

Pickles and Chutneys

Lime or Lemon Pickle I (In Oil)

900g (2lb) green or slightly
   yellow limes or lemons
150ml (¼ pint) mustard oil (from
   Indian stores)
1 teaspoon turmeric
3 tablespoons salt

1 tablespoon saumph (aniseed)
1½ teaspoons crushed mustard seeds
1–2 teaspoons garam-masala
1–2 teaspoons chilli powder
A few green or red chillies (optional)

To fill a 900g (2lb) jar

Cut the limes or lemons into squares; remove all pips, taking care to catch the juice in a jug. If small limes are used, they need not be cut right through. Heat one tablespoon mustard oil in a saucepan; add turmeric, salt and the rest of the ingredients. Mix and simmer for a minute or two; remove from the heat. Then mix or stuff the fruit with this oily mixture; shake well and shift the pickle into a jar. Cover well, and keep in a warm cupboard for a week or a fortnight, shaking it every day, and putting it out in the sun whenever possible. After that, add the rest of the oil so that the pickle is well saturated with it. More oil can be used if necessary; but only mustard oil is suitable for this pickle.

   In India, unripe green mangoes, whole green chillies, young bamboo-shoots, jack fruit, fresh ginger and a variety of other fruits and vegetables are pickled by the above method.

INDIAN cooking

Lime or Lemon Pickle II (without Oil)

900g (2lb) limes or lemons
3–4 tablespoons salt
1 teaspoon turmeric

2 teaspoons garam-masala
1–2 teaspoons chilli powder
A few green chillies (optional)

To fill a 900g (2lb) jar
Cut the limes or lemons into pieces of the desired size, and remove all pips, as described in the previous recipe. Mix in the salt, turmeric, chilli powder and garam-masala. Green chillies (if used) should be washed and drained before they are mixed in with the pickle. Turn into a screw-topped jar and keep the pickle in a warm cupboard or, if possible, in the hot sun for a week, giving it a good shaking every day. When the skins are tender, then the pickle will be ready. Store it, well covered, and shake it every now and then.

This pickle is especially nice with fish preparations.

Lime or Lemon Pickle III

(Sweet Pickle)

700g (1½lb) limes or lemons
1½ teaspoons salt
½ teaspoon turmeric

175g (6oz) demerara sugar
1–2 teaspoons garam-masala
1–2 teaspoons chilli powder

To fill a 900g (2lb) jar
Cut the limes or lemons into pieces of the desired size; remove all the pips, as usual. Mix in the salt, turmeric, brown sugar, garam-masala and the chilli powder; shake well, and after putting the lid back on, keep in a warm cupboard, or in the sun for a week, as directed for the previous recipe.

This pickle will also be ready to eat when the skins of the lemons are reasonably tender. The addition of the sugar seems to give it an unusually piquant taste.

If kept well covered, and shaken every now and then, this pickle should keep for several months.

INDIAN cooking

Gooseberry Pickle

450g (1lb) firm gooseberries
4 tablespoons or more mustard oil
1 teaspoon turmeric
1 tablespoon salt
1 teaspoon or more aniseeds

1 dessertspoon crushed black
  mustard seeds
1½ teaspoons garam-masala
1–2 teaspoons chilli powder
  (optional)

To fill a 450g (1lb) jar

Top and tail the gooseberries, wash and drain them. Heat 1 tablespoon of the oil in a saucepan and very gently fry the turmeric, salt and the rest of the ingredients except for the gooseberries. Remove from the heat, then mix in the gooseberries. Transfer the pickle into a jar with a tight lid and place it in a warm cupboard for a week, shaking it regularly and putting it out in the sun whenever possible. After that, add the rest of the oil so that the pickle is well saturated in oil. Store in a cool place.

Sweet Cauliflower Pickle

About 1kg (2½lb) cauliflower
  (in pieces)
½ bulb garlic
20g (¾oz) root ginger, fresh or
  dried
2 tablespoons mustard oil
225g (½lb) brown sugar
150ml (¼ pint) malt vinegar

1 dessertspoon crushed black
  mustard seeds
2–3 tablespoons salt
1 dessertspoon chilli powder
1 dessertspoon turmeric
1 tablespoon garam-masala
50g (2oz) tamarind

To fill a 1.360 kg (3lb) jar

The pieces of cauliflower should be of medium size; they should be brought to the boil just once, and allowed to cool. Mince the garlic and ginger together, and fry these gently in the mustard oil until golden brown, mash well and keep by you. Mix the brown sugar and vinegar together and boil slowly until fairly thick. Remove from the heat and, when thoroughly cold, mix in it the crushed mustard, salt, chilli powder, turmeric and garam-masala. Add the fried garlic and ginger with the oil; mix well and finally put in the pieces of cauliflower.

Soak the tamarind in a little water, then rub the pulp from the stones; strain through a coarse strainer and add to the pickle. Shake and mix thoroughly, and shift into a large jar. Keep in a warm place for a week, giving it a good shaking every day. At the end of this time, it should be ready.

Carrots and turnips can be used instead of cauliflower. The rest of the ingredients and the method will be the same.

Cauliflower Pickle

(Sweet or Otherwise)

900g (2lb) pieces of cauliflower
100g (¼lb) ginger (fresh or dried)
2 tablespoons salt
1 dessertspoon turmeric

1 dessertspoon chilli powder
1 tablespoon crushed black mustard
    seeds
1 dessertspoon garam-masala

Extra Ingredients

50g (2oz) dried tamarind (not pulp)
1 teacup water for the tamarind

3 tablespoons vinegar
100–175g (4–6oz) brown sugar

Break the cauliflower into 3.5–6cm (1½–2in) long pieces (not too thin). Wash and bring them to boil just once; drain well and cool. If you are using root ginger, it should be soaked in advance, then sliced. Place the pieces in a large glass jar; add salt, turmeric, chilli powder, black mustard seeds (crushed), garam-masala and the sliced ginger. Shake vigorously, cover and keep it in a warm cupboard or in the sun for a few days.

After that, some people like to use the pickle as it is, but to make it more tasty and sweet, the second lot of ingredients are mixed in the following way: soak the tamarind in one teacup of water and remove all the pulp, and pour it on the pickle. Mix the vinegar and brown sugar together, and boil for 2–3 minutes, then add that to the pickle, and shake well.

The pickle should be ready to use after a day or two.

Carrots, turnips and salad cabbage can be pickled by the above method. The cabbage should be shredded and pickled without boiling.

Carrot Pickle with Juice

Kanji

1kg (2½lb) fresh carrots
100g (¼lb) fresh beetroot
4–6 tablespoons cooking salt
4 tablespoons mustard seeds

1 tablespoon garam-masala
1 dessertspoon or more chilli powder
3.4–4.5 litres (6–8 pints) of water

To fill a 1.360 kg (3lb) jar
Scrape, wash and cut the carrots and beetroot into thin, round or 5cm (2in) long pieces. Mix in the salt, crushed mustard seeds, garam-masala and chilli powder. Shake well and then pour in the cold boiled water. Keep this in a warm place for a week. The pickle should be of pale pink colour when it is ready.

The juice is the essential part of this pickle. It should be poured out in small glasses, and served before or after the midday meal.

The beetroot is only added to this pickle for its colour, as a substitute for the maroon-coloured carrots we get in Indian, and if more than the amount given in the recipe is used, it will spoil the taste of the pickle.

Mixed Fruit Chutney

225g(½lb) cooking plums
225g (½lb) cooking apples
225g (½lb) cooking pears or
  apricots
7g (¼oz) root ginger (fresh or
  dried)
12 cloves of garlic

2 tablespoons sultanas
1–2 teaspoons garam-masala
1–2 teaspoons chilli powder
1 teaspoon caraway seeds (optional)
1 dessertspoon salt
350–450g (¾–1lb) brown sugar
225ml (8fl oz) vinegar

To make 900g (2lb)
Wash, dry and stone the plums, and cut them into small pieces. Core and
thinly peel the apples and pears or apricots, and cut them into small pieces
too. If dry root ginger is being used, it should be soaked for a few hours in
advance, then minced with the garlic. Place the cut fruit in a spacious
enamel saucepan, add the rest of the ingredients, including the sugar and
the vinegar. Boil over medium heat for nearly 40 minutes, stirring frequently
with a wooden spoon and crushing the fruit slightly. Remove from the heat
and leave to get thoroughly cold before bottling.

    This chutney is very tasty and it has an attractive appearance.

Gooseberry Chutney

700g (1½lb) fresh, firm
   gooseberries
12 cloves of garlic
50g (2oz) sweet preserved ginger
   or 7g (¼oz) root ginger
450g (1lb) sugar

1 dessertspoon salt
1 teaspoon caraway seeds (optional)
1–2 teaspoons chilli powder
1–2 teaspoons garam-masala
200ml (7fl oz) malt vinegar

Makes enough to almost fill a 900g (2lb) jar
Wash and drain the gooseberries, skin and mince finely the cloves of garlic and ginger (if root ginger is used, it should be soaked for several hours in advance). Place the gooseberries in a spacious, enamel saucepan and add the sugar and the rest of the ingredients, the vinegar last of all. Boil over a fairly low heat for 20–30 minutes, stirring frequently with a wooden spoon to prevent sticking. The chutney should not be allowed to become really thick before it is removed from the heat as it will naturally thicken when cooled. Nor should the fruit be crushed more than can be helped.
   The chutney should be stored only when it is thoroughly cold.

INDIAN cooking

Green Tomato Chutney

900g (2lb) firm green tomatoes
15 cloves of garlic
15g (½oz) root ginger (fresh
  or dry)
450g (1lb) sugar, preferably
  brown

450ml (12fl oz) malt vinegar
1½–2 teaspoons garam-masala
1½ teaspoons caraway seeds
  (optional)
1 tablespoon salt
1½–2 teaspoons chilli powder

To fill a 900g (2lb) jar
Rinse, dry and cut the tomatoes into small pieces; skin and mince the garlic
and ginger. If dried root ginger is used, it should be soaked for a few hours
in advance and then minced. Place the tomatoes in a heavy enamelled
saucepan, add sugar, vinegar and the rest of the ingredients. Cook these
over medium heat for 50–55 minutes, stirring frequently with a wooden
spoon and crushing the tomatoes slightly after they have become soft.
Remove from the heat and cool thoroughly before pouring into jars.

The chutney should be stored in a cool place.

Black or Red Currant Chutney

350g (12oz) firm red or
  blackcurrants

6 good eating dates (stoned and
  cut small)

To fill a 450g (1lb) jar
Apart from the fact that black or red currants are substituted for the
gooseberries, and the dates are added, the ingredients for this chutney are
the same as for the Gooseberry Chutney (page 179). The method of
preparation is the same, and the cooking time over medium heat is from
15–20 minutes.

Mint Chutney

Podina Chutney

6 medium-sized spring onions
1 teacup ready-to-use mint
2 medium-sized minced green
   chillies or ½ teaspoons chilli

   powder
1 teaspoon salt
1 teaspoon sugar

½ teaspoon garam-masala
1 tablespoon dried pomegranate
   seeds (anardana)
   (available from Indian
   stores)
1 dessertspoon ground mango or
   1 tablespoon lemon juice

For 5 people
Wash the onions, throwing away only the tough green leaves. Then wash the mint under running water, and mince these two things, and the fresh green chillies together. Put them in a mortar, add salt, sugar and garam-masala, and crush for several minutes with the pestle. Remove and set aside on a plate. Sort and rinse the dried pomegranate seeds, and crush them in the mortar separately, then put the half-prepared chutney back in the mortar and crush and mix thoroughly. Lastly add the ground mango or lemon juice, and mix once again. Transfer to a glass dish and serve.
Mint chutney will keep for a day or two, but is tastier when freshly made.

Coriander Chutney

Dhania Chutney

The ingredients and method for this are the same as for mint chutney, except that coriander is substituted for mint and the pomegranate seeds are omitted.

INDIAN cooking

Tamarind Chutney

Imli Chutney

100g (4oz) of good dried tamarind
About a teacup of water
1 tablespoon sugar

1 teaspoon salt
1 teaspoon garam-masala
½ teaspoon chilli powder

For 4 people

Rinse and soak the tamarind in some of the water for a few minutes, then rub it well with your fingers to separate the pulp from the stones and fibre. Gradually add the rest of the water. Put this mixture in a strainer with medium-sized holes, placing a small bowl underneath. Press the mixture through the strainer with a wooden spoon, so that all the pulp comes out from it. The dry fibre and stones should be thrown away. The pulp will be fairly thick and will contain small bits of tamarind which are quite harmless. Add the rest of the ingredients to the pulp. Mix thoroughly and the chutney will be ready.

This chutney will keep for only a day or two, and is served with many Indian savoury delicacies.

INDIAN cooking

Index

INDIAN cooking

INDIAN cooking